WELL LIVED

SALLY CLARKSON

HARVEST HOUSE PUBLISHERS
EUGENE, OREGON

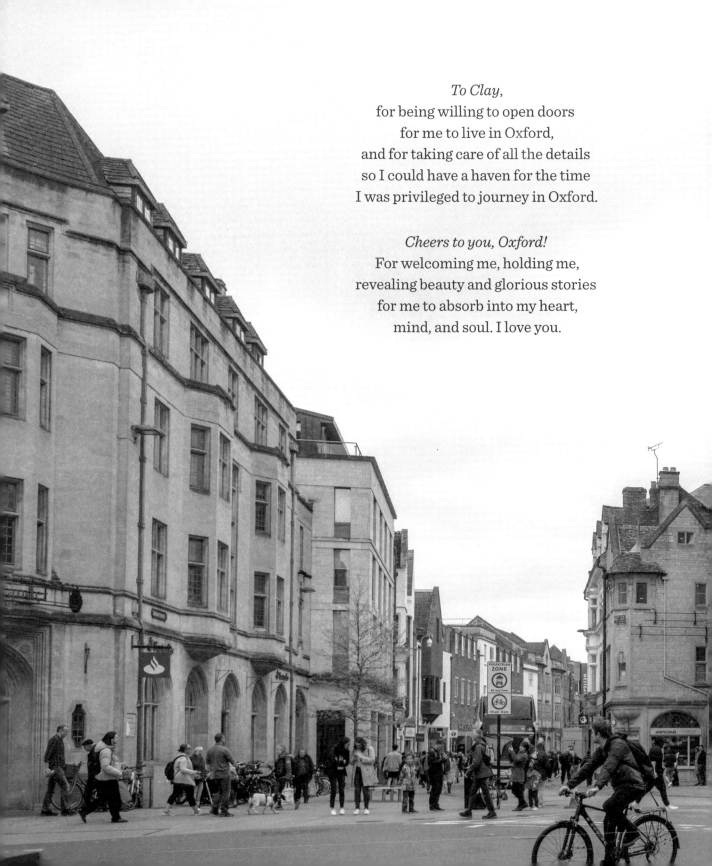

To Clay,
for being willing to open doors
for me to live in Oxford,
and for taking care of all the details
so I could have a haven for the time
I was privileged to journey in Oxford.

Cheers to you, Oxford!
For welcoming me, holding me,
revealing beauty and glorious stories
for me to absorb into my heart,
mind, and soul. I love you.

To my Precious Lord,
who has held my hand, led me, comforted me,
taught me His ways, given wisdom, and
companioned me with grace,
mercy, and love each step of my journey.

The purpose of life is...
to be useful, to be honorable,
to be compassionate,
to have it make some difference
that you have lived and lived well.

RALPH WALDO EMERSON

CONTENTS

LEAVING A LEGACY OF A WELL-LIVED LIFE

Blessed is a person who finds wisdom,
And one who obtains understanding.
For her profit is better than the profit of silver,
And her produce better than gold.
She is more precious than jewels,
And nothing you desire compares with her.
Long life is in her right hand;
In her left hand are riches and honor.
Her ways are pleasant ways,
And all her paths are peace.
She is a tree of life to those who take hold of her,
And happy are those who hold on to her.

PROVERBS 3:13-18

Five short years ago, I melted into the folds of a deep, squishy couch, stuffed into a tiny living room in an old Oxford flat. My oldest daughter, Sarah, lived there with her husband and baby girl. She was holding my first grandchild, Lilian, a few months old, gently bouncing her in the air, resulting in giggles and smiles.

"Mama, what do you want to be called as a grandmother? I think it should be something unique and creative that reflects your personality and what you like."

*Who has put wisdom in
the innermost being,
Or given understanding
to the mind?*

JOB 38:36

As it happened, the two years before, our family had been working our way through a British drama series called *Lark Rise to Candleford*. This television series was loosely based on a trilogy of semi-autobiographical books by Flora Thompson during the latter years of the 1800s. Set in Lark Rise, a small rural village, delightful tales were spun about the country folk who often interacted with the more upscale, prosperous folk in the larger neighboring town of Candleford. Each episode brought heart-touching, humor-laced, folksy stories, opening windows to family life, community gossip, festivals, and celebrations, as well as connection made through the varied adventures.

A beloved character, Queenie, was a wizened old woman who was the sage matriarch of Lark Rise. With witty charm and a warmhearted countenance, she shared her insight, experience, advice, and encouragement from the domain of her homey house on the top hill of the town. Her homespun remedies brought healing; her recipes, comfort and satisfaction; her love, hope and cheerfulness of heart. She always had a story to tell that intrigued her listeners and invited them to apply the wisdom of the tale. The people of her village trusted her because of her years of serving her community with great affection, friendship, and insight. Ever charitable, extending guidance and support, she ruled the small village from the humble kingdom of her home.

As we were talking, Sarah suggested, "Mom, you are like Queenie, benevolent, distributing goodwill, cheer, and wisdom to all who come into your sphere. I think your grandchildren should call you 'Queenie.'" Honored by her gracious words, I became Queenie to all the little people birthed by my children.

Later, my younger daughter, Joy, said, "I was the one who suggested Queenie, don't you remember?" While there were varying recollections about who bestowed the name, there was agreement that Queenie in some way defined my approach to shaping a well-lived life. After all, my name, Sally, means "princess," and it is only right that at age 70, I would graduate from princess to queen, thanks to my girls.

Historically, a good queen brought about a life-giving influence as she considered herself a steward, responsible for the long-term prosperity and flourishing of those who were within her realm. Her significant role affected the legacy of her life, the story she would live, the heritage she would leave. It also influenced the legacy of her family, community, and world in the rare times a queen gave herself to the full task of all that had been entrusted to her. Being a steward over human beings can have great impact over generations if the faithfulness and generosity of the queen is purposefully focused and lived out over a lifetime.

In time, I began to realize how much "Queenie" represented to me the better aspects of my womanhood—the picture I had in my heart of becoming royalty when I was adopted by God, and the idea that I was His servant and He my king and companion. I have rather liked embracing this role actively in the lives of my family and friends. And I was honored to play my part in His plan well and purposefully.

Wisdom and Womanhood

Decades before I was Queenie to the grands, I had longed for companionship and wise input throughout all the seasons of my work, marriage, parenting, and ministry so that I could play my part well. Yet often, as a wife, mother, friend, and professional writer, I was figuring it out alone, without much mentorship or direction. This earlier lack of guidance stirred in me a growing desire to be an encouraging companion to others who also longed for friendship that called them to their best selves. I wanted to validate their efforts to write a great story with their lives

For if we live, we live for the Lord.

ROMANS 14:8

through steadfastness, love, and grace. I became a treasure hunter, gathering insight and knowledge along the way so I would be equipped to help others find direction, meaning, courage, and contentment.

I came by much of my experience and wisdom simply by living my life long enough and trying at every turn to trust God as my confidant, guide, and strength. Now, reviewing my life comes with a sense of awe and surprise. So much has happened in this full and multidimensional life of mine. At this point in time, I've been married 43 years, birthed and educated 4 children, written 30 books and worked with 8 different publishers, moved 24 times—9 times internationally—and lived in 4 countries, spoken to hundreds of thousands of people, worked in missions and ministry for 51 years, and hosted

But if any of you lacks wisdom, let him ask of God, who gives to all generously and without reproach, and it will be given to him.

JAMES 1:5

23 national conferences for 80,000 people. I have lived through surgeries, heartbreak, stress, car wrecks, and personal failures, but I have also experienced great joy, unconditional love, deep friendship, excellent teaching from others, and the intimacy of walking with God as my companion for 53 years.

I deeply love being a matriarch—a woman learning to live into my capacity, slowly becoming confident of the powerful influence I could wield in the places I live and in the lives of my people. My influence would come through serving them in love, cultivating goodness, nurturing their spirits, and passing on hard-earned lessons. I found that by giving my life, laying it down, so to speak, others could

draw life and encouragement from me. This role became the most profound and fulfilling endeavor of my life.

Unexpectedly, serendipitously, the opportunity to spend months at a time in Oxford came to me in my late 60s. Oxford became a place I would sort of "sabbatical" for some months over a few years to be near my grandchildren, to celebrate life with my own children, to reflect on life, to explore the stories of others in days gone by, to store wisdom in my soul and enjoy my people. After 50 years of working hard and long through ministry, my husband said, "You need some months of escape where you can ponder life, enjoy

your grandchildren, and breathe a bit." Wanting to share from the stunning adventures I had, the interesting places I grew to love as I walked the cobbled streets and pondered life over long cups of tea, I decided to place this book into the context of times I spent in what became my beloved Oxford.

Learning and understanding that every woman has potential to embrace her own story, to become "queen" over her own domain, to work hard to leave a legacy of wisdom, love, gratitude, and grace emerged as a message while I walked through parks and meadows and wrote in my journal. Women, I believe, are amazing creatures and have the ability to civilize the world, to influence generations by generously pouring out love, training the very character and souls of the next generation and persevering through great trials and challenges while coming out resiliently.

Be very careful, then, how you live—not as unwise but as wise.

EPHESIANS 5:15 NIV

The book of Proverbs in the Bible hails the wondrous attributes of women. Proverbs 31:10 even says, "Her worth is far above jewels," a veritable treasure in the times of Solomon who wrote this book before Christ. And Proverbs 4:5-9 reveals the many blessings of getting wisdom:

> Get wisdom, get understanding;
> do not forget my words or turn away from them.
> Do not forsake wisdom, and she will protect you;
> love her, and she will watch over you.
> The beginning of wisdom is this: Get wisdom.
> Though it cost all you have, get understanding.
> Cherish her, and she will exalt you;
> embrace her, and she will honor you.
> She will give you a garland to grace your head
> and present you with a glorious crown. (NIV)

Early in my adult journey, the Word of God became my instruction for all of the pathways of my life. What I discovered was that true, foundational wisdom was not relative, subject to whim and mood. God had provided leadership, pathways to follow, truths to enact in order to live well, flourishing over a lifetime. And yet I realized that biblical wisdom is not prescriptive, but often open-ended, able to be practiced in many different ways, in a variety of contexts and life stories, through unique personalities, cultures, and circumstances.

Every woman has potential to embrace her own story, to become "queen" over her own domain, to work hard to leave a legacy of wisdom, love, gratitude, and grace.

I began to picture my own heart, soul, and mind as a treasure chest where I stored up wisdom, insight, and perspective through all the twists and turns of my life. And from this treasure chest, I would draw insight and instruction for others if it might help encourage them along their way. And others would draw from me what I had stored in my treasure chest of life. Eventually I pictured my children's hearts as treasure chests in which to deposit wisdom and truth.

Living into my role as queen, guardian, protector, lover, and provider for those in my own realm, I sought to actively pursue opportunities where I might bring hope into discouragement, faith into doubt, love where there are broken or lonely hearts. Understanding that life is filled with tragedy in a fallen, broken world has prepared me to have compassion for others and a capacity to companion those who are grieving or struggling. I consider it a privilege. I have longed for sympathy and comfort in my own life, and I hoped to give some small bit to others.

Pointing out the beautiful fingerprints of God, the dimension of the world He crafted for our pleasure, the gifts of love hidden in our relationships, and that light is always more powerful than the darkness are some of my heart treasures I stored.

My hope was that I could guide, inspire, support my own beloveds through the passages of their own lives. As I matured over time and moved more gracefully into my role, I grew in my desire to come alongside other women, in the realm of influence God had opened up (and men—especially my own boys!) to provide some leadership and encouragement about what I had learned. And so began years of books, conferences, blog posts, and podcasts.

Time to Grow and Become

As the message of this book simmered in my imagination over months, I realized it was part memoir about how I have evolved and grown through the years. I grew to become a sort of queen in my own realm as I acquired understanding and insight over seven decades. This book is also a continuation of that early desire to come alongside others and open a window to life so they won't feel alone in their journey. I hope to pass along more freedom, more grace, more beauty in the pages ahead.

A few days ago, I came upon a grandchild of mine who was singing at the top of her lungs and dancing around the living room, and I joined in enthusiastically. It is an image of what I hope you will find in the pages of this book: encouragement to experience life in its fullness, to enter into the joy that is offered, even amidst the mundane. My offerings from my life in photos are meant to show some of the amazing places Oxford brought my way as I explored, pondered, and breathed in peace. I relearned ways to celebrate life, to soak in the beauty that every day holds.

Every man's life is a fairy tale, written by God's fingers.

HANS CHRISTIAN ANDERSEN

Pressures, darkness, and struggles of life will come and go. Yet the secret of learning to see hidden beauty that surrounds us and to experience the gift of friends and loved ones is to cultivate the wisdom to enjoy the moments you have been given each day. This is the beginning of a life well lived.

I have no formula or agenda I think all women should follow. But I offer some of my stories and experiences while in Oxford these past years. I hope that it might bring grace, freedom, and encouragement to you, a fellow traveler on this road to a well-lived life.

I pray you will give yourself time to grow and learn, and grace when you falter or make mistakes along the way. I hope that you, like me, will find the freedom to live vibrantly into your own unique story, especially suited for your personality and for your circumstances. Life for most of us is a long journey, lived over decades. We have time to grow, to become, to access what is deep within our hearts to "be," and we will find the poise with which to live a meaningful and fruitful life.

Women have an endless capability to civilize life; to pen or verbalize great messages of God's truth; to fulfill potential in ourselves and others intellectually, spiritually, emotionally; to be astute in a variety of areas of skill and expertise. We are great comforters, able nurses, gardeners of souls and soil. We are musicians who celebrate the symphonies of life and artists who create, gather, and share beauty.

To live well and honorably and justly are the same thing.

SOCRATES

We were not left without leadership. God has granted us secrets of wisdom and understanding in His Word, the Bible, while also gifting us with wide ranges of how to embody this wisdom. There are wise ways to follow, with much freedom to apply them uniquely within the context and diversity of our own stories. Becoming queen of your own domain and becoming the ruler over your life story are lifelong pursuits and will be unique for each woman, and can provide deep soul satisfaction in the pursuit.

I hope that you, like me, will find the freedom to live vibrantly into your own unique story, especially suited for your personality and for your circumstances.

I never could have imagined that I would have the privilege of living in Oxford, United Kingdom, at this season of life. The gift of time each year in Oxford has afforded me the ability to ponder and reflect on my life and the importance of living with determination to fill my days with what really matters. Oxford is the place where I have tied together many thoughts, experienced beauty, and dwelled on wisdom from those who have gone before me. And all of this done while sipping tea, walking cobbled streets, meeting lovely friends, and opening my eyes to new places, experiences, and fun.

In my journal I have written of obstacles overcome, wisdom gained, and discoveries made about the truth and mercy that flow beneath this one life of mine. This book reflects some of the lessons I have learned and the grace I have experienced in this life-giving place and in this life-giving season. I treasure my days as Queenie as I kiss the heads of my grands and walk the parks and canals and meet people from all over the world. These moments are rich because I am living them as well as possible with the full understanding that being loving and grateful through each day is the key.

It is my hope that this length of path we walk together will validate your own vision for your life and validate your great worth as a woman who brings light, beauty, and wisdom to your own people and places. Let us link arms together in dear friendship and enjoy a stroll through Oxford side by side. I cannot wait to share my favorite places, my delights, my ponderings, and my joy. May every step encourage your well-lived journey. Cheers, my friend.

I have written of obstacles overcome, wisdom gained, and discoveries made about the truth and mercy that flow beneath this one life of mine. This book reflects some of the lessons I have learned and the grace I have experienced in this life-giving place and in this life-giving season. I treasure my days as Queenie as I kiss the heads of my grands and walk the parks and canals and meet people from all over the world. These moments are rich because I am living them as well as possible with the full understanding that being loving and grateful through each day is the key.

ONE

CURATING DELIGHT

The LORD makes firm the steps
of the one who delights in him;
though he may stumble, he will not fall,
for the LORD upholds him with his hand.

PSALM 37:23-24 NIV

Mama! You won't believe this! I was granted a full scholarship to get my Master of Theology at Oxford. Would you consider visiting for a while? I'm going to need help when the baby comes so I can attend seminars each week."

That phone call from my daughter was the start of an adventure that would lead to many others in the years to come. My husband, Clay, and I were delighted to journey "across the pond," as they say, to be supportive of Sarah and her husband, Thomas. This was to be my first grandchild. We knew this was a once-in-a-lifetime opportunity to be present at the dawn of this sweet baby's life.

We began planning for our journey to Oxford immediately. Clay located a small, old house just down the street from Sarah's flat, and I started the task of packing what we might need. I had been to the UK many times before, but now I could stay there for six months during her term and take in its treasures in a new way. So, as I packed, I dreamed of sipping tea in a lovely cottage with friends, being surrounded by fascinating historical architecture, having life-changing conversations with the intelligent students who attended Oxford to become world changers. I envisioned strolls through vibrant gardens in the sunshine with flowers abloom in every color. Maybe I would even sense the spirit of Jane Austen, hear the whispers of C.S. Lewis's stories, live among Tolkienesque images, and dine at a table in the Great Hall in the Harry Potter movies, a real dining hall at Oxford's Christ Church.

Yet a differing reality awaited us, one that would teach me to watch closely for delight even in—especially in—the middle of imperfect circumstances.

Alas, not every moment was to be a scene out of a romantic novel, as we often expect of places we have dreamed of living. During those first months in my charming cottage, we had an infiltration of ants that had to be dealt with. Laying ant traps all over our first floor was something I would learn to do strategically as a warrior against the critters in my home. Next was an onslaught of giant black spiders that crawled sneakily above my bed to drop down onto my covers without warning. Tales of rats in the walls came from a friend down the street, apparently a risk for houses so near the canal. Oh, so that's why so many cats rambled around our small garden. The shower leaked and had to be fixed. Adding to that, I had an accident and sliced my right eye four levels down in my cornea and had to go to London for ten weeks of treatment to save it. Yet, I had learned over seasons that there is no perfect place, no perfect person or family or job. It is in learning to practice joy and delight despite the difficult contexts of our circumstances that we find deep soul satisfaction.

An effort made for the happiness of others lifts us above ourselves.

LYDIA M. CHILD

Needless to say, I was learning to lower my expectations and accept the limitations of living in Merry Old England. I was determined to place my attention on the many blessings and the reason for my being there. My family has always been my greatest joy, and here I was, in another country, able to play a role in one of the most important seasons of my daughter's life, and our own as soon-to-be grandparents.

The Grace of Delight

Anticipating the arrival of the new baby, Sarah, her husband, and I attended a tour of the area's well-known hospital, which had amazing facilities and birthing centers. They touted wonderful, well-appointed rooms with every comfort imaginable for mothers and infants, constant attendance by midwives, and low lights to soothe babies. This visit filled our heads with the idea that her experience would be sublime. However, when Sarah actually went into labor, it was on the night of "the beast from the east." Snow and ice covered

the roads; taxis were unavailable; freezing temperatures made the roads dangerous. Not long after midnight, a kind neighbor was willing to brave the weather and drive Sarah, Thomas, and me to the hospital.

When we arrived, the scene was wrought with havoc. Many of the staff had been there for 36 hours and every room was filled with a laboring mother. Not exactly the dream birth story. Yet room was made for Sarah, and when baby Lilian appeared, healthy and robust, we were all grateful for this tiny gift. Infant smiles and coos, darling antics of discovering the miracles of life from this tiny baby provided so much pleasure the stresses prior to her birth were soon forgotten. The delight of this living miracle saved the day. The blessing far exceeded the burdens. The heart riches of holding my first grandchild in the following months made up for it all.

Delight has a way of giving us grace. It mercifully clears from our mind the strife required to get us through what might at first seem like impossible circumstances. By developing the practice of gratitude, we create a habit to minimize the routine difficulties of every day while also maximizing the joys of each day. When we trust that God has us and is holding us up, even in the middle of a storm or in the middle of human chaos, we can find our delight in our personal story of His faithfulness.

Few delights can equal the mere presence of one whom we trust utterly.

GEORGE MACDONALD

God Knows Our Heart Desires

Throughout the year, when I would walk to Sarah's house, I passed by the most amazing cottage. I called it "The Fairy House" because it seemed to have been transported from a magical land. Most of the homes in the neighborhood hailed back to the 1860s, when there was a local factory where many worked and used the canals to transport their goods. But the fairy house stood out from these utilitarian homes. It had wood-framed windows, flower boxes, and an inviting bench in the driveway surrounded by large half-barrels filled with flowering plants. Lining the property were tall trees with billowing branches gently blowing above the bench. Apparently it had been in decline, but a visionary architect had restored the whole house and added charm and character.

Every day I paused a moment to take in the view of this special home, and every day my heart felt a twinge of longing for its wonder. I made a personal declaration for no one

but God to hear: "If I ever come to Oxford again, I would love to live there for a while." I told no one else of this desire.

> When we trust that God has us and is holding us up, even in the middle of a storm or in the middle of human chaos, we can find our delight in our personal story of His faithfulness.

A year later, we were back living in the States, and Clay and I considered how great it could be to live, once again, near Sarah, Thomas, and their growing family. *Wouldn't it be fun to take some months to travel in Europe and enjoy our near retirement age and restore our vision for what our lives would hold?* With only tourist visas, we had to come in and out of the country. So we searched for a suitable place to rent and looked at almost 90 places. The prices were high, and the flats were not very suitable to our desires. We always cherished places where we could extend hospitality by hosting Bible studies, dinners, and family gatherings.

Sitting on our deck in Colorado, we would sift through endless rental property postings. One day my son Joel, home for the summer, said, "I found the cutest place for you."

And wouldn't you know it? It was *the* fairy house. When we called to check on it, we found it had already been rented out. I kept it to myself, but as I prayed, I felt that sometime, now or later, the Lord would provide us with such a place. We had experienced a very taxing and trying year, and I felt in my heart He was going to give us a welcome reprieve.

Sure enough, four weeks later, on the day we were supposed to sign a contract for a different flat, Clay looked online and found that our fairy house was up for rent again. I say "our" because in my heart, it was surely ours. We called and the office staff told us that the man who had rented the house had to cancel because of circumstances in his family. "We were just going to post it online in a few minutes, but if you rent it right now, we will not advertise it to others and you can have it."

Not all moments are seeming miracles like this, but I was quite sure the Lord had granted me a desire of my heart. And His timing couldn't have been better; COVID-19 was about to make its appearance on the world stage. We were to live in that special house, and it became a haven for all of us. We had far more room than any of the other homes would've provided. There were even two drawing rooms so I could have a small sitting room and Clay had the other as his own visiting space and small office upstairs.

Great joy, especially after a sudden change of circumstances, is apt to be silent, and dwells rather in the heart than on the tongue.

HENRY FIELDING

Delight saved the day…and so much more during that time.

The garden area in front of our home was an unexpected gift amidst the challenges of the pandemic when gatherings with anyone beyond one's immediate family were relegated to outdoors. Having such a personal outdoor place on our home's property was nearly unheard of in our Oxford area. We celebrated many magical events as a family and with friends. And Clay and I had some of the most delightful times of our whole marriage in this home that seemed to embrace us with affection.

*Delight yourself
in the LORD;
And He will give you the
desires of your heart.*

PSALM 37:4

Planning for Delight

About the time the pandemic's impact was winding down, our beloved fairy house was to be sold, and we, once again, faced the daunting task of finding a new place to call home. Yet, by this time in life, nothing surprised me. I had learned to put away fear, or the pretense that I could ever control life. Over these seven decades of my life, I have learned to leave my burdens in the hands of God and to be thankful every day, acknowledging His presence. Learning to celebrate even the small details of life, to be grateful for beauty and blessing, and to be patient during trials have been lifelong lessons.

It is never easy to accept what a broken world can hold for us, but it is particularly hard to do when we're young. Many of us can recall specific incidents when reality hit us the hardest and we needed to find a way to see the light and joy God lavishes on us even when we experience disappointment.

I had to discover how life in a fallen world could indeed bring heartbreak and times of devastation—and that God would companion me during those seasons with sympathy, strength, and love. I also learned that I could bring light into the darkness. I

could be a provider of hope, support, and beauty for my friends and family. Just as they could offer to be that for me. Experiencing the joy of celebration amidst disappointment became a valued conviction and a real way of seeing the circumstances of my life with seasoned eyes.

This lesson of delight crystalized in my mind in another era. Many years ago, I was engaged in student ministry overseas. I found myself living through a very bleak winter in Communist Poland and sustaining the difficulties and rigors of a Soviet-dominated country. Small quantities of fresh food were available only occasionally. A police state ruled over the people and created much fear. The dark, cold days had depleted our emotional reserves. My cherished roommate and dearest friend, Gwennie, and I decided to take a vacation to England. We desperately needed a break.

Credit cards were not commonly used at this time, so we had to cash some checks to bring money with us to pay for our fun, food, and expenditures. We had the equivalent of about $750 between us, which seemed plenty for our three-week trip in the 1970s.

We arrived and spent a couple of wonderful days relaxing, being with friends, eating great food. Then Gwennie suddenly came down with a terrible toothache. A visit to the dentist was a necessity. For several days, I sat in the dentist's waiting room as he drilled, cleaned, filled, and injected smelly medicine into her sore mouth. This incident kept us from touring the city and celebrating times of leisure on our much-anticipated vacation. Because she had no dental insurance for England, we had to combine our resources to pay cash for the bill, which used three-quarters of our saved funds. We would have to be really frugal for the remainder of the trip if we were to make it.

As it happened, my birthday was at the end of the week after the expensive dental emergency. Gwennie said, "I want to take you out to tea for your birthday."

"I don't think we have enough money to do that," I protested.

Yet she insisted that a cup of tea was not an extravagance but a necessity, and we found a suitable place to celebrate the day. As we were talking, sipping, and munching a piece of cake, suddenly a barely audible *beep, beep, beep* sounded from an alarm.

Much to my surprise, Gwennie smiled from ear to ear, clapped her hands together, and said, "Present time!" Out of a bag she had been carrying on her shoulder she retrieved a lovely little wrapped box. A charming carved jewelry box for my earrings was inside. I was so very surprised, tickled that somehow she had managed to get me a little

*I delight greatly
in the L<small>ORD</small>;
my soul rejoices
in my God.*

ISAIAH 61:10 NIV

gift during this challenging week. I wondered where the money had come from.

A few minutes later, her travel alarm went off again. Again she squealed, "Present time!" And again, another gift appeared. This happened three more times! Now everyone in the café was watching us with anticipation of what would happen next. All of us were laughing, conversing, and having a very sweet time of camaraderie. Finally I asked Gwennie, "How in the world did you pull this off with no money?"

She smiled broadly, and with a twinkle in her eye, she said, "I knew it was going to be your birthday, so I got the gifts over the last month, wrapped them, and brought them with me in my suitcase because I wanted to celebrate you." She paused. "You know I love to be prepared. I planned delight for this day ahead of time to show you how deeply I value our friendship."

Her preparation to surprise me, delight me, made that birthday celebration far sweeter than anything I could have imagined. But she *had* imagined it amidst the dark days and stress of the mundane in Poland…and she made it happen even though our resources were so limited. You and I have opportunities to imagine and plan for delight in our everyday life. Preparing to be a celebrator, a worthy lover, a cheerful friend, an encourager, a lifesaver requires practice. It is an ability we cultivate by noticing ways to be present for others with simple offerings of time, fellowship, thoughtfulness, gifts, and gestures that say we see and appreciate them.

Directing your vision toward hope, finding it as the lens with which you see your life and the people in your life, provides the possibility to create joy, pleasure, and goodness for those who move in the realms of your world even when life is chaotic.

You and I have opportunities to imagine and plan for delight in our everyday life...It is an ability we cultivate by noticing ways to be present for others with simple offerings of time, fellowship, thoughtfulness, gifts, and gestures that say we see and appreciate them.

Look upon us, O Lord,
and let all the darkness
of our souls
vanish before the beams
of thy brightness.
Fill us with holy love,
and open to us the
treasures of thy wisdom.
All our desire is
known unto thee,
therefore perfect what
thou hast begun,
and what thy Spirit has
awakened us to ask in prayer.
We seek thy face,
turn thy face unto us
and show us thy glory.
Then shall our longing
be satisfied,
and our peace shall be perfect.
Amen.

AUGUSTINE OF HIPPO

Because Gwennie planned her celebration, the reality of our challenges on our trip faded to the background. In that moment and now when we recall that trip, the focus is on the joy, the fun, the good memories. I stored up the wisdom to understand that I, too, could become an emissary of delight and goodness for those God placed in the spheres of my life. Contentment, thanksgiving, and creating delight in mundane days are not necessarily parts of our human nature, but beautiful habits that give grace to our lives will develop as we practice them over and over again. Such practices reflect the Holy Spirit breathing joy through us. What we practice we become—my experiences in Oxford and my life journey have taught me this.

When we notice God's work in our lives, we witness how the harder times can provide the deepest opportunities to develop patience and gratitude. The smallest joys are magnified when we've plodded through a season of discontent or difficulty. These experiences prepare us to be an influence for joy. They shape us to be an agent of encouragement, of gratefulness, of delight-making, not only for our own lives, but for the lives of those around us who need to be comforted, helped, and lifted up.

I believe that life is given us so we may grow in love, and I believe that God is in me as the sun is in the color and fragrance of a flower, the Light in my darkness, the Voice in my silence.

HELEN KELLER

TWO

GOOD MESSAGES, GOOD HABITS, GOOD STORIES

All Scripture is inspired by God and
beneficial for teaching, for rebuke,
for correction, for training in righteousness;
so that the man or woman of God
may be fully capable, equipped for every good work.

2 TIMOTHY 3:16-17

Three-story, redbrick Victorian homes along a tree-lined street provided a charming backdrop for meanders through the neighborhoods of my beloved University Parks. Imagined scenes of long-gowned women pushing their babies in large, black prams accompanied my thoughts as I moved toward the floral fields and swaying branches of centuries-old trees just ahead. Visions of distinguished professors holding formal dinners, seen through the 15-foot-high glass windows framing elegant dining rooms, discussing profound issues of science, literature, history, and math, reflected stories I had heard repeated often.

Experiencing the beauty of University Parks has been a vital, life-giving aspect of my time in Oxford. It's been a gift to share this with my family as well. There were months when I would meet my daughter Joy here at the end of the day. Though she was a student at St. Andrews in Glasgow, Scotland, she studied for a while in Oxford because it had a bigger library. She was diligently

reading and writing her PhD dissertation, and I was working on yet another message or podcast outline or reading a great story. We had "our bench" by the duck pond where we would meet and talk about everything we had pondered, studied, and read that day. Just swimming in the profound thoughts of her research gave me a new sort of education. What a delight it was to now be learning from the one who had once been my student.

Later, I discovered my own bench, one hidden in the heavily wooded area where I could bring my journal along with my cup of coffee from Brew, one of my favorite coffeeshops, and an almond croissant, a specialty of Oxford. Here, I would ponder life under the gentle, cool breezes blowing through the trees and write down my thoughts about what I had been learning and thinking. This practice centered me. And there in the quiet, my thoughts gathered and clarified under the tall maple, a sequoia, and chestnut trees where literally thousands of people had sat and pondered life since the park was designed in 1864.

Often I would think, *If someone had told me when I was young, starting out as a writer and missionary, I would have the privilege of visiting Oxford for stretches of time in my mid-60s, meeting with women from all over the world while also sharing experiences with members of my family, I would have thought it was mere fantasy.*

Yet here I was in England, where I was investing so much time growing and also learning from deep thinkers—men and women from very differing contexts than my own. My heart for people from so many war-torn or oppressed countries grew larger. My sympathy for others who had come from difficult backgrounds grew deeper. My gratefulness for the opportunity to keep growing and learning in such a place was overflowing.

One day, while sitting on my bench, I was overcome by a sense of God's providential leading and presence in my story. This life season was made more dear, more significant because it was built on a lifetime of immersing in His messages and drawing near to His heart.

What It Takes to Follow God

"How did you get to live in Oxford?" people queried through letters, messages, in person. "I want to live there."

Each person has their own story of faith to live and their own path to obedience to give themselves over to God's kingdom work. Choices are made each day that shape their own destiny to live exercising their own gifts. The fingerprints of God are all over each of our lives, and He ordained that as we live into our capacity, our lives would be full to overflowing. When we read of Abraham's life, it is said, "By faith Abraham, when he was called, obeyed by going out to a place which he was to receive for an inheritance; and he left, not knowing where he was going" (Hebrews 11:8).

This had been true of my own life: following God over many years, often not knowing where my obedience would require me to go or the demands it would place on my life. Many times I was led to countercultural decisions. Yet I counted on the fact that if I followed hard after God, my life would be filled with meaning. I had faith in His leading to work in me and shape me to become more like Christ and to mature more, and that He would companion me each and every step.

It had all started years before when I was a college student in Texas.

"Sal!" my Southern friend said to me over canned split-pea soup. "I think God is going to really use you profoundly in your lifetime. Go get 'em, work hard, live passionately. I believe in you, Sal!" (No one else ever got away with calling me that nickname.)

I was so hungry for my life to have meaning, I took her at her word and ran forward into the next years with the gusto of a very sincere, albeit inexperienced heart.

Early on, I learned a word that gave leadership to my decisions through many seasons and gave direction to the light inside me. I had *capacity*: innate, God-given dimensions of talent, life, and goodness within the dictates of my own personality and strengths to access through all the days of life.

Discovering that I had the ability to exercise this capacity through my talents, skills, dreams, self-discipline, and choices, as well as to stretch in my ability to learn new things, fueled my determination to live into the potential I had been granted. The belief that all women have great capacity fueled many faith decisions I made in my life to take risks, to grow more knowledgeable, to stretch in my abilities to become astute in life.

May my soul thirst for Thee, who art the source of life, wisdom, knowledge, light, and all the riches of God our Father.

BONAVENTURE

The fingerprints of God are all over each of our lives, and He ordained that as we live into our capacity, our lives would be full to overflowing.

Learning that wise people copy wise people, I saw most relationships as opportunities to grow, learn, and understand new contexts. Consequently, I wanted to love people well and learn from their lives. Through pathways of my life, I learned to invite people in, seek to find their worth, and grow in understanding and wisdom by asking questions. Seeking knowledge of people and of God's way and world became my way of life.

The second word that motivated me was *agency*: the ability to take action and to make decisions to influence the flow of my life by acting decisively in the direction of my desires and potential.

Learning that I had agency showed me that I did not have to be a victim of my circumstances but had the power to move beyond my failures or frailties. The growth was deeper than merely having the ability to "get over" hard things; I would grow stronger and more authoritative to make progress and mature in character and skill in my life.

Your word is a lamp to my feet And a light to my path.

PSALM 119:105

As a young woman, I could face challenges empowered by this sense of agency. I trusted God had given me a sound mind that I could fill with His truth and Scripture, which gave me freedom to move into the directions that most aligned with the personal abilities and goals God had set before me.

Every person has agency to write the story of their lives by making choices that lead them in the direction of what they hope life will be. We each rule over a kingdom of sorts—our lives, our friends, our work, our family.

I exercised my agency, my will, to stretch toward seeking truth and understanding in order to live in the endless capacity God had given me to grow.

Meeting Him Within

Before my Southern friend cheered me on and before I had a personal faith, I was an 18-year-old freshman in college who cried out to my then unknown God, "If You are there, please let me know You." I repeated my prayer every night. I told no one. One day a soft knock on my dorm door surprised me. A quiet-spoken, friendly young woman greeted me. She worked with a campus ministry. To make a long story short, she shared a survey with me, told me a little about herself, and then she ended her conversation with me after about a half hour explaining the generous love of Christ and how it had transformed her world.

When she explained how knowing God meant I could deal with the ways I fall short to live a perfect life, a light went on. And as she described how I could find purpose and meaning by knowing God through His Son, Christ, her words utterly touched a deep longing inside. That is when I started my relationship with God. It was as though sunshine shone inside my heart and mind.

From that moment on, I carried the desire and maintained the perspective to know how to use my capacities and exercise my agency and will to spread this sunshine in every aspect of my life. My influence over the people God brought into my life would be driven by the light, goodness, and beauty I had received when I had come to know His love.

This doesn't mean my life was free from devastation, disappointment, or darkness throughout the years. But the new light in me compelled me to look for the sunshine, to dance to His song. And over time, I could clearly see my life purposes were to shed light in the darkness, offer hope in disappointment, and bring healing into devastation.

The grass withers and the flowers fall, but the word of our God endures forever.

ISAIAH 40:8 NIV

I was fortunate because right at the dawn of my belief, a friend would meet with me and teach me how to understand and read the Bible. I was so very surprised at how much I hungered to understand God's truth and develop my personal theology—an understanding of who God was and what God was like.

My habit has been to return to the place where I first found Christ, to see my heart attitudes as the place I worship God by choosing to hold out His light and goodness, to believe in the reality of His light even when life feels dark. Each time I return to this internal place of commitment, I have found Him there waiting to give me courage, provide strength, build compassion, and teach wisdom.

The new light in me compelled me to look for the sunshine, to dance to His song.

The habit of coming to God every day, taking time specifically to seek Him, to listen to Him, to ponder His ways and engage in His truth, is the action that has shaped my life most profoundly.

I hardly need to say I was not perfect, and some stressful crisis seasons found this habit not happening every single day. But over many years, as I read my Bible, I began to see foundations of life shaped by the wisdom I was learning and the understanding of God's ways I was gaining. I found that reading God's Word and praying were essential to my ability to continue one more step in the direction of my own ideals, giving me fuel for my strength when life was exhausting. It is a habit I want to help others learn how to develop.

When we are serious about God, we must be serious about investing in Him. Others need the truth He teaches us. More voices and messages invade the sound waves of our brains today than ever before through social media, movies, and other online outlets.

We are living in a melting pot of cultures, where all religions and values and morals drift together and are said to be equal; where all varieties of moral behavior are validated and find acceptance; where television and film and the internet smudge the clear borders of truth every day, promoting violent behavior and dark themes. The call to mentor others and teach our children has never been more important or necessary.

We must not underestimate the draw these voices have in our lives and those of our children as they become young adults and begin to make decisions that will determine the outcome of their futures. They must know the voice of the real, true, loving, living God, not just platitudes of moral rules. Only real wisdom and Scripture will do.

Building Unmovable Foundations

We build the foundational belief system and understanding of God's nature in ourselves and our children's minds one day at a time, one brick at a time. To have a strong standard of truth invading and speaking to our invisible thoughts, our minds must be filled with thousands of teachings of Scripture so our brains will have a go-to place when we are making decisions about their lives.

As so many women have heard from me over the years, "In the absence of biblical conviction, people will go the way of culture." In other words, if we have not been taught, trained, and instructed in the wisdom of God's Word, and if we have not learned to pray and become familiar with His voice, then we will listen to the loudest voices, the ones most elevated by the world. If a woman has not invested her mind to engage in true biblical principles, she will not have the ammunition in her soul to fight the values and voices of culture.

A heart that is filled with and informed by biblical convictions does not just happen. It is shaped intentionally over many years, day by day, circumstance by circumstance. It all starts with a willingness to pay the price of commitment, time, and preparation over a lifetime of good and godly habits that renew us, our relationship to God, and our ability to shine truth into the lives of others.

During our time in Oxford, as I developed relationships and people began to know my family, many women from vastly different backgrounds, countries, and ages would ask to meet with me for advice or input. Often we would walk together along the canals near my home, stroll through the University Parks, or meet for a meal or coffee, opening deep talks about what was on their mind. From these individuals I eventually gathered a group of women for a Bible study in my home, which turned into two groups over time.

Therefore everyone who hears these words of mine and puts them into practice is like a wise man who built his house on the rock.

MATTHEW 7:24 NIV

Sometimes I would visit their homes, bringing flowers or baked goods and cards of encouragement. Weekly I would make meals and invite women over so we could deepen our connection. These practices were acts of keeping the joy of His reality alive in our relationships.

A heart that is filled with and informed by
biblical convictions does not just happen. It is
shaped intentionally over many years, day
by day, circumstance by circumstance.

My whole life's story had been transformed by knowing the truth of God's never-ending love and care for me. Always God companioned me, encouraged me, and gave wisdom and insight to me as I needed it through the seasons of my life. Because of His faithfulness, it has been my long-held desire to share with others about what God's love has done just as the woman from a campus ministry had shared with me so long ago.

In this city rich in both story and history, I had a full-circle experience in my own story. I recognized the things I had prayed for so many years before were still pulsing through the minds and hearts of others with similar longings. Women from all over the world came across my path with the same hopes and desires I had felt as a young woman in college. As a result, I started two mentoring groups—one to married women, one to graduate students.

Know that the greatest things which are done on earth are done within, in the hearts of faithful souls.

ST. LOUIS DE MONTFORT

*Lord, thou hast
given us thy Word
for a light to shine
upon our path;
grant us so to meditate
on that Word,
and to follow its teaching,
that we may find in it the
light that shines
more and more until
the perfect day;
through Jesus Christ
our Lord.
Amen.*

JEROME

The sunshine that was inside my heart was an organic, natural part of my life that spilled into all areas. And so, acting in light of this gift of love I had been given, Oxford has been a place where I could live authentically and naturally from the wellspring of His love flowing through me to those precious ones He brought into my life. Oxford, for me, has become a sacred place to experience and share the message of His love. Always, those I have had the privilege to work with enriched my life as well.

*Keep good company, read good books,
love good things and cultivate soul and
body as faithfully as you can.*

LOUISA MAY ALCOTT

THREE

BRINGING LIFE TO THE WORLD

May the LORD cause you to flourish,
both you and your children.
May you be blessed by the LORD,
the Maker of heaven and earth.

PSALM 115:14-15 NIV

Every Monday morning I rise earlier than normal, drink my tea, and read my Bible. Next, and just as important, I plan what sticker books I will pack in my bird tote (the one with a variety of birds painted on the material) where I keep markers, stickers, coloring books, and small puzzles, always adding new ones. This is the morning I meet my sweet grands and Sarah in a café down the street. Now, years after we welcomed the first grandbaby in Oxford, Sarah's family has grown to three little ones and a baby. There is always so much joy when we are together.

We greet one another with plenty of hugs and kisses and then get down to the business of ordering our favorites. Juice and *pain au chocolat* for the littles, a flat white coffee with *pain aux raisins* for me, and an apricot pastry for Sarah. And for about an hour the children color, tear out stickers, share their thoughts and adventures of the week, and ply their talents to the crafts from my little bag.

We wile away our time chatting about everything that is occupying their enthusiastic minds, talking about fairy dresses, favorite books, and dragons.

My mama heart is full as I hear their stories, both real and imagined (though I don't always understand every word), and as they take in my tales. Every moment I can I am investing lots of love and kisses into their memory banks. There are numerous times when I am in Oxford while Clay holds down the fort in Colorado, so I absorb these sweet experiences to share with him when I return to the States.

After our café time, we don coats and wellies (rubber boots) and brace ourselves for what is usually a cold, rainy, or foggy day. On previous Mondays, we have explored grave-yards and hunted for bluebells, a flower with majestic blue-purple blooms; but eventually, inevitably, they ask to go to Queenie's house, my own little home.

My temporary English flat is not by any means a perfect haven for littles. The compact rooms are awkwardly shaped and allow little space for the active play of rambunctious children. So to remind my grands they are always welcome in my humble dwelling, I have two cupboards below my bookshelves that house Legos, shape sorters, a couple of games, some puzzles. Because my grands know they have their special place in my home to hold their treasures, they are assured they belong here.

My small patio and the garden just off the kitchen serve as places of play and discovery. They have provided the tiny backdrop for plastic egg hunts, well beyond Easter, and for afternoons spent picking the wildflowers growing in random clusters to put in vases "for Mama." We've watered plants along the fence because, even in cool weather, it's fun to help green things grow. And no matter what form of play we've delighted in, always, always Lilian eventually requests, "Queenie, may I have a cup of tea?"

It is no wonder these times and these people are so dear.

All That Is Good

As I reflect on the many years of my life, I can say beyond a doubt that my role as mother, and now grandmother, are the most profoundly important and meaningful ones. The idea that God would entrust us with human beings to parent, to shape, protect, teach, and provide for, took me many years to appreciate for what it is: a strategic role, a privilege, and a design from God's heart.

Any mom knows that the gift of being a parent comes with many significant responsibilities. I was unprepared, untrained, and honestly, had not given motherhood a lot of thought back in my single years. At almost 31, never having changed a diaper, never knowing a mom who had nursed her children, and not even knowing how to hold a baby, I was heading into a great unknown— this thing called motherhood!

The living, the living—
they praise you,
as I am doing today;
parents tell their
children
about your faithfulness.

ISAIAH 38:19 NIV

And yet, when my first baby was born, it was not the overwhelming sense of responsibility or inadequacy that hit first but the incredible wave of unconditional love. Even now I can tear up remembering the first days of becoming a mother—the surprise of it, the mystery, the utter miracle of bringing a life into the world.

These are my first memories recorded in my journal:

> *As I first cradled baby Sarah, I was afraid I would drop her or hurt her somehow. I held her tightly in my embrace with a sense of wonder and reverence. Dark-blue eyes the color of blueberries stared up intensely in the direction of my voice. Two matching bruises on her forehead where forceps had been used to help her emerge from my womb gave a battered look to her tiny face.*

Dripping dark strands of hair framed her face of pearl-white skin. At that moment, I was starstruck with my little newborn, first child.

I was not expecting the pure awe that would flood my heart the moment she arrived and was gently placed into my arms. For a moment, I had her alone in the finally quiet hospital room. As I was holding her gingerly so as not to harm her, it was as if God was whispering to me:

You are holding eternity in your arms. This little one is a miracle, a gift from Me. Will you cherish her and love her so that when she grows up, she will believe that I love her? Will you be responsible to shape and fill her mind with the best stories so she will always believe in heroes? Will you whisper to her the secrets of My ways, teach her what is true, give her a place to grow strong and a sanctuary in which to celebrate all that is good in life so that she will fill the treasure chest of her soul with all that is good, true, and beautiful?

Truly, for me, it was a defining moment. In one brief twinkling of time, I imagined what I would provide, teach, honor, and encourage throughout the countless days of our many future years together. All this opportunity and hope came wrapped in this little seven-pound gift. I began to understand that I would be a conductor of life for this little one born dependent on my guidance, love, and direction. God gave me, as her parent, a key to free the potential locked in her heart, soul, and mind.

We Are Life Givers

When I read in Genesis that Eve was called "the mother of all the living" (3:20) or "life giver" (AMP), I had an "aha" moment. I had never been taught what the Bible said about women. But the more I read and studied, the more I breathed in the vast design God had granted to women.

Her children arise and call her blessed; her husband also, and he praises her.

PROVERBS 31:28 NIV

With a defining name of "life giver," I cultivated a broad vision of myself, and of all women, who could bring life to all aspects of our world. Women have been designed with a womb in which they might conceive, grow, and birth human life. Also, I see that with the name "life giver" pronounced over us, women with or without children have special abilities to express this life in many ways. Our brains are wired to integrate all aspects of our journey. As "life givers," we bring life to relationships as we foster heart connections; life to the spirit as we uphold the value, faith, and purpose of each person; and life to the mind as we engage and develop the intellect.

Specifically, though, for me, the conviction about the strategic role of motherhood as a full expression of life giving grew into a passion and call on my life over the years. Since I became a mother, I have studied the Bible about the issues of motherhood and have written many books that underline the profound importance of motherhood.

Another entry in my personal journal:

> *Mothers are the civilizers of nations because they teach and enlighten, train and inspire their children in all aspects of life to live into their potential. Mothers model serving Christ in front of them every moment of every day by showing and telling them how to love God, to have a heart that values righteousness. Through this amazing work, children will hopefully become adults who serve God actively and who bring His kingdom to bear.*

From the moment our children arrive in our homes, we are teaching them how to see the world, what to consider important, what to seek, what to love. Mothers have the opportunity to form home and family life in such a way that God's reality comes alive to our children each day. The meals, conversations, and prayers we foster become the training and our homes, our presence, and the world are the training grounds.

As these tiny human beings find themselves swimming in the love, affection, and tenderness of their mothers, they will flourish and grow. When they are talked to, engaged with, invited to explore and ponder, they cultivate a lasting love for learning and grow intellectually and spiritually. The whole world becomes their laboratory where they learn and develop, all because there was a person conducting the order and pattern of their purposeful days.

We bring life to relationships as we foster heart connections, to the spirit as we uphold the value and purpose of each life, and to the mind as we engage and develop the intellect.

Every child born into the world is a new thought of God, an ever-fresh and radiant possibility.

KATE DOUGLAS WIGGIN

Not all women will become mothers. Not all women will bear a child. But all can bear witness to life in Christ through the expression of mothering and nurturing in their friendships, in counseling, ministry, marriage, work relationships. Since I did become a mother, I have come to realize that embracing God's call to the duties of motherhood and grandmotherhood over the years doesn't diminish—but actually grows—my abilities to use my gifts, strength, and training in a broad sense to fulfill a part of God's design.

By being accountable to God for the human beings entrusted into my arms, I had to grow in the direction of the ideals I wanted them to understand and emulate. And

this personal character development influenced so many other realms of my life: my work habits, my writing and speaking, my willingness to accept the difficulties and bring light into the dark chaos. What you practice in small areas of life impacts what you become in other areas.

After years of learning to live sacrificially in order to be a life giver, the mantle of motherhood brought me great peace and capacity for all of my journey. My own interests were stretched by the many inquiries and studies of my children, my education was broadened, my writing was enhanced by the countless books we read together, and my mind became stronger in and through ideas shared, discussed, and even challenged by my family.

When you look at the ways you give, consider all the ways you in turn receive life. It's as though there is a constant replenishing from the original Life Giver so we can give from a place of abundance and gratitude without hesitation. All that God wants for us and for our lives is expanded, deepened when we are willing to pour into the people He places in our care.

A particularly sweet delight filled me as I also gained a vision for bringing the life spark of creativity to my personal world: infusing the rooms and rhythms of my home with color, comfort, resources, beauty, traditions, celebrations, hospitality, and caregiving.

> All that God wants for us and for our lives is expanded, deepened when we are willing to pour into the people He places in our care.

By taking my children and grands to museums, concerts, libraries, homeless shelters, fruit and veggie markets, church, walking paths in nature, I learned to develop their interests in a world of art, music, curiosity, ideas, work habits, service, and pleasure. With deep gratitude, I have watched them adopt their passions in their unique way for their lives as they grew into the values we shared from the beginning. Now my grandchildren accompany me and my daughter to these varied places, and we all celebrate this wide world of discovery and adventure together.

No language can express the power and beauty and heroism and majesty of a mother's love.

EDWIN HUBBELL CHAPIN

Experiencing all the good and all the growth buoyed a positive attitude. Now, instead of seeing fusses and messes as irritations in my day, for instance, I am more likely to see these as opportunities to continue training my children, and my grandchildren, to be peacemakers. I slowly, patiently (at least that is my goal!) help them learn to be responsible for their own messes. Instead of resenting the interruptions in my schedule, I am more likely to accept them as divine appointments.

Say to mothers, what a holy charge is theirs; with what a kingly power their love might rule the fountains of the newborn mind.

LYDIA H. SIGOURNEY

Queens of Our Domain

I was in England when Queen Elizabeth, the longest ruling monarch, passed away. I have read books about her, watched movies, read articles from people with whom she lived and worked. It seems she had been given a deep sense of her stewardship to care for those in her domain.

My friend and I talked about these ideas and the Queen's life as we pondered what it looked like to consider motherhood as a sacred truth from God. When Queen Elizabeth was crowned during her coronation, she was anointed with oil by the Archbishop of Canterbury in a solemn and sacred ceremony, where she took an oath before God. She knew she was set apart to serve. Throughout her life, Queen Elizabeth continued to serve God with her whole heart, as she was raised to believe the role of the monarch was to bring light, beauty, and truth to the world. The vision of her role was spoken to her often by her father, the King. She had a sense of the historical and spiritual value of her role.

When a child is born, so is a mother. In a sense, mothers are set apart, holy, for the work of giving life to the children entrusted into their hands. And while swaddling precious new life, we aren't anointed with holy oil right there on the spot, but we are anointed with the Holy Spirit for the work ahead. On the days that it feels like a burden

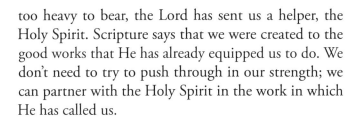

too heavy to bear, the Lord has sent us a helper, the Holy Spirit. Scripture says that we were created to the good works that He has already equipped us to do. We don't need to try to push through in our strength; we can partner with the Holy Spirit in the work in which He has called us.

Holy Spirit,
giving life to all life,
moving all creatures,
root of all things,
washing them clean,
wiping out their mistakes,
healing their wounds,
you are our true life,
luminous, wonderful,
awakening the heart
from its ancient sleep.
Amen.

HILDEGARDE OF BINGEN

Just as Queen Elizabeth believed her role as a monarch was to bring light, beauty, and truth to the world, mothers were designed by God to do the same for our households. Women are uniquely fashioned in the likeness and image of God to curate goodness and dispel chaos; to kindle hope and foster faith. We are the beauty bringers and soul shapers of our homes and our communities, and for those God places in our domains. That is, if we accept the weight of the crown of responsibility.

Believing and accepting the role of life giver to children brings me deep, satisfying blessings. Three littles, 5, 3, and 18 months, and a newborn, remind me again and again how profoundly meaningful my reign as a mother and grandmother is.

We are the beauty bringers and soul shapers
of our homes and our communities, and
for those God places in our domains.

Not only have my children become my dearest friends in all the world through the years of our being mother and child, but now I have a new community and a second opportunity to give and receive love to the little people who call me Queenie.

I have come to see that all women have the potential to shape the elements of a beautiful life in a variety of ways and to carry out their service to God by doing so. We live most fully into our potential as we come to understand ourselves as life givers and co-creators with God, and when we realize the birth of a child is only the beginning for both of those roles and the legacy we shape along the way.

For we are God's handiwork, created in Christ Jesus to do good works, which God prepared in advance for us to do.

EPHESIANS 2:10

The Crown of the house is Godliness.
The Beauty of the house is Order.
The Glory of the house is Hospitality.
The Blessing of the house is Contentment.

OLD INSCRIPTION

WE ARE THE LIGHT BEARERS

You are the light of the world.
A city set on a hill cannot be hidden; nor do people
light a lamp and put it under a basket,
but on the lampstand, and it gives
light to all who are in the house.

MATTHEW 5:14-15

On a side road in Oxford near the canals sat our little fairy house. The one we were blessed to dwell in during the pandemic, when we and others needed its beauty and light. With flowering bushes surrounding the driveway and window boxes overflowing with blooms, it was a treasure of a home amidst many old, creaky places. A bench that whispered "welcome" sat just outside our front door. Sometimes even strangers would come and sit for a few minutes on this bench for peace, quiet, and a short rest because it bordered the road outside our home.

It was as though an angel had designed a haven just to bring delight to a season that could've been dark and discouraging. Touches of light and wonder could be found in every space. A floral stained-glass window faced the winding steps to our cozy bedrooms. A hidden inner garden with a bubbling fountain provided a tiny courtyard of privacy, a perfect place to steal away with friends for a cup of tea and a time of quiet reverie. And perhaps my favorite space was

a charming room at the front of our house. It became my sanctuary for creativity, a place to imagine how to bring life to our days, a place of soul rest, a sort of altar for my times with the Lord. I often gathered and read to my little grands here so we could revel in stories across from the fireplace aglow with a cracking blaze.

At the front of this room, a bay window and a small ledge faced the outdoor street where my neighbors passed by all times of day. In the winter, the sun set after four in the afternoon, so I would light several candles placed on the ledge and plug in a string of fairy lights to give people passing by a little "Hello. How are you? Here is some light to warm you." One day while walking to a nearby market for groceries, I ran into a neighbor who remarked, "Are you the one who has candles burning for us morning and evening in your window? It makes me feel happy, welcomed to my own home." Each morning after that, when my neighbor left his house, he waved at me through my window.

The simple things are often what allow us to be light bearers, to bring warmth and connection to others.

Agents of Grace

As a little girl, I loved Christmas lights. I would walk around the neighborhood with my little dachshund named Happy and breathe in the beautiful, colorful lights. We lived in a tiny subdivision, and everyone prided themselves on their Christmas lights. Some red, green, or multicolored. Some were pure white, twinkling like stars. The lights left an impression on my little-girl heart of magical, mystical possibilities, of a world where fairy tales could come true, where hopes did not disappoint.

Created by God to be image-driven human beings, since almost everything around us is perceived with our eyes, it's important that we give our children and our adult hearts images that live on in our imagination. We are agents of Christ's grace and light and have the privilege during our time on this earth to sing and teach and tell of His ways and light until the victory banquet when we see Him face-to-face.

When my children were small, we spoke of Jesus as the light coming into a dark world, but we also wanted them to have images and experiences that would live on in their memories forever. Traditions are a way to cast light on young ones' hearts. Many

In the same way, let your light shine before others, that they may see your good deeds and glorify your Father in heaven.

MATTHEW 5:16 NIV

years ago, with the desire to create a meaningful Christmas Eve, Clay and I started what we call a "Shepherd's meal" to honor Jesus's birth and presence for all, from the poor shepherds minding their flocks who were the first to welcome the Christ child to the kings who would follow with their regal gifts.

The humble evening of simple food and setting was made magical the moment we turned off all the lights in the house and lit 20 candles. Replicating a time when there was no electricity, our candles gave off a bit of light even as the torches and stars filled the dark nights with sparkle. It was glorious. We told the story of the people who lived in darkness having seen a great light. The wonder went deep into our children's hearts, so much so that as they have become adults and our circle of family, friends, and acquaintances has grown, this time of reverence and ritual is cherished and requested.

Our basic cuisine became a family favorite. We served potato soup with warm, buttered herb bread and pungent cheese amidst the darkness and twinkle of candles which lit up the room. We set the stage, so to speak, of the evening the angels came announcing the birth to the humble shepherds with the glory of stars, angels, and proclamation.

We were made to be image keepers.

We are agents of Christ's grace and light and have the privilege during our time on this earth to sing and teach and tell of His ways and light until the victory dinner when we see Him face-to-face.

Darkness threatens so many sacred places in our times. Marriage is being attacked. Children are not valued. Violence is pervasive, and still there are wars and rumors of wars. The battle rages. Yet we have a conqueror, a warrior on our side, one who has already been victorious. He is with us. And we may champion alongside Him with confidence and sing His praises with joy.

Our Unique Light

Each year I determine several themes I will choose for the focus of my heart's eyes. This year I chose to look for light, to observe it, to note its beauty. When in my Colorado home, I would notice the sunrise shimmering in the aspen trees near my front window. In Oxford, I walk a short pathway next to my canal most nights to see the sunset playing through the woods and shining on the water. And I remind myself, Jesus is the light. He dances in all my places; He wants to bring the light of His truth to my heart to give hope to my weary days. Light reflects the essence of Christ to me, so I notice light to remind me He is everywhere.

Because of my determination to look for light, I have noticed it casting shadows upon trees and the leaves seeming to lean forward to catch a glimmer of sunlight. I pay attention to sunrises and sunsets. I look for light because He is light, and it causes me to worship Him for bringing me out of darkness. Honestly, because I made this commitment, light has captured my attention many times a day; each instance whispers to my heart, "He is here; you are not alone."

Imagine my delight when I took the train to visit a dear friend in London and she said, "I have a surprise for you," and whisked me off to an amazingly exquisite chandelier shop. Beautiful light and cascading reflections shimmered everywhere. A friend of hers from church owned the shop, famous all over England as a place to find the most elegant light fixtures. Her showroom was literally lit by hundreds of bulbs from chandeliers that had been curated because of their historical significance. The shop owner had become a collector of lights, another image of what we are supposed to do—collect the light that Jesus scatters in our lives as an encouragement to ourselves when we especially need His light.

"This one is from Lady Diana's family home."

Grace comes into the soul, as the morning sun into the world; first a dawning; then a light; and at last the sun in his full and excellent brightness.

THOMAS ADAMS

"The large one in the corner came from the winter castle of a famous duke."

"The small, dainty one with the winding leaves and flowers was lodged in a convent where the inhabitants were known for cultivating beautiful gardens and delectable meals. It was a gift to them from royalty."

"The grand one in the middle was treasured by Queen Victoria; she placed it at the entrance of one of her favorite rooms."

"Each piece shows light in its own unique way. Each one tells a unique story. Yet all bring light to their worlds."

Just like all of us, I thought. How that captured my imagination!

We each bear light through our own unique stories and relationships, and each of us can bear light into the nooks and crannies of our worlds. What if each of us determined to leave light with everyone we came across: with our children, our friends, our husband? But to do that, we must be in an intimate relationship with the true source of light, Christ.

Are there negative things that creep into my life? Discouragement, exhaustion, feelings of inadequacy or blame, and a critical attitude sneak in from time to time. But because of my commitment to grow in light, I notice the darkness when it wants to enter. I close the door, refusing to let it in, and I seek to move my heart and thoughts to the beautiful power or energy of the light of Christ. He said, "The people walking in darkness have seen a great light" (Isaiah 9:2 NIV).

We each bear light through our own unique stories
and relationships, and each of us can bear light
into the nooks and crannies of our worlds.

The disciples who faithfully followed Christ came mostly from the cross section of common people. They were oppressed by the constant cruelty and rule of the Roman soldiers. Most were poor because of the high taxes that were exacted from them each year and were oppressed by the legalism and demands of the Pharisee-led faith system. In short, they were "sheep without a shepherd" (Matthew 9:36).

Imagine the fire that was lit in their hearts when Jesus brought them onto a mountaintop with Him, seeking to deeply encourage His closest companions and friends. He looked them in the eye and said, "You are the light of the world" (Matthew 5:14). His words elevated their sense of worth. Do you speak words that elevate your friends' and your family's sense of worth—they are the light, the goodness, the beauty that God has chosen to bring to this world at this time.

When Jesus spoke again to the people, he said, "I am the light of the world. Whoever follows me will never walk in darkness, but will have the light of life."

JOHN 8:12 NIV

These words must have struck the disciples profoundly. Us? How can we be light? We're so common. We're just normal human beings who fuss and struggle to have enough food to eat, to care for our elderly, to parent our children, to make ends meet amidst a long life—but Jesus's words lift us in purpose: You, you followers of Mine. You are the ones who bring the light of God's love and truth and beauty into the reality of the lives of others who long for comfort, forgiveness, help, truth. And so His words still lift us today.

Illuminated Souls

God's Word also brings light to our dark souls when we need to keep going, to cherish what is good in the world when we are tempted to be discouraged. Feeling overwhelmed is normal in this broken world. But knowing Jesus gave us the light is what we need to hold fast to what is good, true, beautiful.

I have curated several passages in Scripture that regularly bring light and hope to my soul in different moods and circumstances. I hope they do the same for you.

I am not bound to win, but I am bound to be true. I am not bound to succeed, but I am bound to live by the light I have.

ABRAHAM LINCOLN

1. If God is for you, who can be against you? Romans 8:31

The light of encouragement fills our minds when we remember that we are not alone, that we are not without help. God is for you—*for you*. He wants you to succeed. He wants to work in your life, your work, your home. When God's Spirit is working in our midst, He will take our fish and loaves, all that we have to give to Him, and together with Him, our labor becomes enough. He is for you, sweet one, if your heart is to serve Him. He has compassion on you, He knows your weariness, and He is your champion.

2. There is no condemnation for those who are in Christ Jesus. Romans 8:1

Light floods our hearts when we live by a standard of grace, not perfection. I wonder why we have the illusion that we are supposed to be perfect. Don't be so hard on yourself! You will not ever be perfect or do everything right—not now, not next week, not even when you are 70, like me. I keep waiting for an age when I will not be petty or self-absorbed. And to live in guilt because you have blown it or yelled in anger or made mistakes is a big drainer.

3. Then he lay down under the bush and fell asleep. All at once an angel touched him and said, "Get up and eat." 1 Kings 19:5 NIV

Light infuses our attitudes when we take time for rest and restoration. Elijah was so weary from spiritual battle that he despaired of his life, wished he hadn't been born. But God knew he was exhausted, battle worn, and weary, just as we are at times. The first thing God did when Elijah poured out his heart to Him was to put him into a deep sleep. Next, an angel touched him. Physical touch—a hug, an embrace, a hand massage, a real massage—is healing. I love that God's angel touched Elijah and brought him physical comfort. God didn't give Elijah a lecture; instead, the angel fed him.

Sometimes we have been going for so long without a break, we start breaking down. A wise woman will learn her limitations and learn to say no so that she does not live in a constant state of exhaustion. You can only hold so many ideals at once, so be sure to hold on

THE
VOL. VII.
THE
VOL. VII.
1916
THE
1913
THE
1915

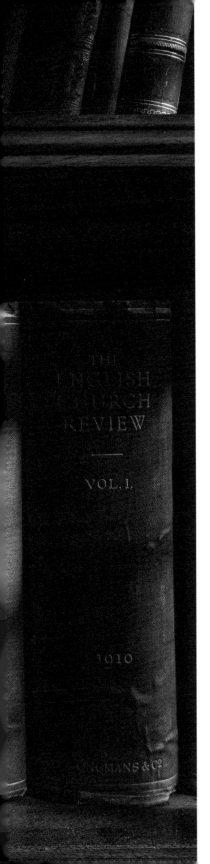

to the ones that matter. And do what you are best at doing; don't compare your life to someone else's. You might need to start out your new beginning with sleep, a loving touch, nourishment, gentle movement, and then take time to ponder and plan.

We are not just minds and hearts; we are bodies with limitations. If we overexert ourselves, we will crash and burn. When others are taking from us 24/7, we must wisely learn that taking care of ourselves is essential to our emotional, spiritual, and physical well-being. This season, if you are tired, be sure to take a break that refreshes your body, mind, and spirit. You deserve to be cared for, so even if you have to plan for it yourself, set in motion those times for wellness.

From within or from behind, a light shines through us upon things, and makes us aware that we are nothing, but the light is all.

RALPH WALDO EMERSON

For many years, I waited for someone to give me permission to take a break, but that didn't happen. Finally, I took responsibility for my own happiness so that I could be happier and stronger for my kids, Clay, and friends on this long-term journey.

4. Walk with the wise and become wise, for a companion of fools suffers harm. Proverbs 13:20 *NIV*

Light fills our emotions when we find the care and wisdom given in friendship. You might need some inspiration, some help, some counsel, some perspective. Find someone older, more experienced, and wiser to meet with, or make time for friendship with someone who calls you to your best self. Sometimes this is easier said than done. I have found that when I give up my pride and pour out my heart to wise people, I usually find compassion and often find help.

For many years, my mentors were books. I was always hunting down volumes written by those who were older and wiser. More insightful. I committed myself to learning and growing every year.

The desire to gain knowledge and learn from others is our invitation to be teachable and willing to change when we need to. Find wise people, books, conferences, a church, the Word of God, and glean wisdom from them. Just decide to grow and progress every year.

Life is a long journey, and we will always need the light of His companionship and encouragement every step, every day. Store up His love and truth daily that Jesus might be to you the light of your world, and you will not walk in darkness but have the light of life.

May we be collectors of light and bearers of light so that we shine forth today. May we walk in the light of His counsel as a way of life, as rhythmic as breathing through all the moments of our lives.

Open wide the window
of our spirits,
O, Lord, and fill us
full of light;
Open wide the door
of our hearts,
That we may receive
and entertain Thee
With all our powers of
adoration and love.

CHRISTINA ROSSETTI

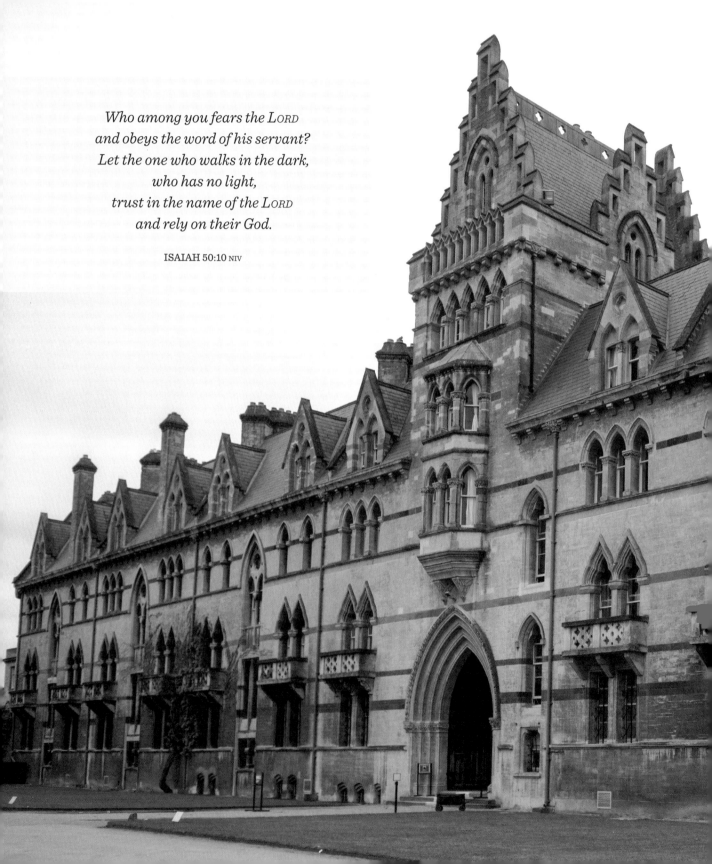

Who among you fears the Lᴏʀᴅ
and obeys the word of his servant?
Let the one who walks in the dark,
who has no light,
trust in the name of the Lᴏʀᴅ
and rely on their God.

ISAIAH 50:10 ɴɪᴠ

FIVE

THE PLACE OF WELCOME

By wisdom a house is built,
And by understanding it is established;
And by knowledge the rooms are filled
With all precious and pleasant riches.

PROVERBS 24:3-4

Every seat on the plane was occupied, including the seats to the right and left of me. Enduring the 10-hour flight felt almost more than I could take on this particular day. I felt squished between two strangers, restless and unable to sleep, and fidgeted actively the whole flight. International travel is not as easy for me as it used to be when it was an adventure in my younger years.

Next was emerging from the plane slowly behind the crowds of others who longed for freedom. Lugging a heavy small suitcase stuffed to the gills with necessities I might not be able to purchase in my little neighborhood store and a tote bag overloaded with my computer and must-have books made my shoulders sag.

My watch that measured my steps told me I had walked .6 miles to reach the passport security room, which was crowded with hundreds of travelers. Next, after a half hour of moving as snails toward our checkpoints, was the baggage hall. My suitcase is almost always one of the last ones to come down the baggage slide. Finally, lugging my three bags onto a cart, I walked the half mile to the next car park area to find my ride. Blessedly, my patient friend, Jacqui, often arrives to drive me the final hour and three minutes to my home in Oxford. She is my travel elf.

Living in a foreign country and traveling multiple times a year brings with it many challenges or, shall I say, opportunities to stretch toward contentment and to learn a new level of flexibility. Always I am glad to be home whether that happens to be in England or Colorado.

As we arrived in town and made our way closer to my Oxford home, I began to breathe in peace because I anticipated what was ahead. Texting my son Joel, "Home in ten minutes," gave warning to my people that they were about to be invaded by my friend and me.

A simple "Welcome Home" sign had been scrawled and taped to the house. As we opened the door, acoustic Celtic music wafted in our direction, and we left the luggage in a corner to deal with at a later time. My senses were greeted with all that resonates as "home!" in my heart. The smell of buttered toast and warming almond pastries invited us to the kitchen. The table was set with our lovely dishes we had discovered on eBay, candles had been lit, a bowl of fruit cut, and Clay made us fresh cups of tea while Joel encouraged us, "The cheesy eggs are almost finished. I thought you might need a bit of sitting, sipping, and eating to face the day." And so we did.

I could not have hoped for a better welcome home.

The wisest of women builds her home, but folly with her own hands tears it down.

PROVERBS 14:1 ESV

A Vision of Home

As a seasoned woman who has lived in over 20 homes of differing designs during my marriage, I have cultivated my taste and preferences. And as a curator of all things life-giving and beautiful in my home, most of my rooms in my family home in America are very intentionally decorated. With great care I chose shades of wall paint, art, photographs, mirrors, lamps. I created comfy, private corners. Couches and chairs are arranged to allow for intimate conversations, times of friendship, heart-shaping discussions. Even now in my Oxford home, which lacks many of the traits I would choose, I have tried to create these spaces for connection.

I am a lover of light and of windows that have a view toward nature, a look outward to the world. My narrow row house now (not the fairy house) built during the Victorian period has windows that look out on a local pub and cars parked up and down a street busy with taxis, commuters, and cyclists. Between driveways, I see the rubbish bins (garbage cans) of other homes lined up. Not the ideal view I have come to value.

Many of the houses on my street are more than a century old, and over the years various owners have renovated, restored, or modernized the homes, including ours. At some point

in the past, the kitchen in our house was renovated, creating an area for a dining table and lovely windowed doors that look onto my wild garden. My eyes lit up the first time I saw this part of the house. It was the outward view I craved and the calm area my heart desired.

Soon after we moved in, I secured a small Persian rug, ordered a two-person couch, bought side tables in a secondhand shop, and made a cozy space by the kitchen windows for sitting and drinking tea together with family members or friends.

My husband and I regularly sit here to end our day, to talk about life, to enjoy our friendship. This kitchen/living room space is also where my children and friends choose to relax when we are having a moment together.

I built my vision of home over the years; yet even early on as a young woman, I saw myself as the designer and artist of the structures under our shared roof. Clay also brings his taste and heart to the organization and feel of rooms and the colors and artifacts we choose to place in our surroundings. Together we became designers not only of the interior spaces shaped for comfort but of the structures of traditions, routines, values, and experiences we would cherish and grow from together. And always my desire was to create a place where my family and guests would feel cared for, celebrated, and loved.

Our homes could have a little space for withdrawal and quiet, and even a small garden could offer some distance from noise.

THOMAS MOORE

Meaningful Treasures

The Google dictionary definition of *home* is: "The place where one lives permanently, especially as a member of a family or household." While this vague definition is true, home is *so* much more than a shelter where we simply eat, sleep, and gather. It is a welcoming refuge, a safe haven for our children and those we welcome in for beauty and rest.

A home that nurtures us is one that invites us to delight in food that comforts, to cuddle up to familiarity, to participate in routines reinforcing a sense of security, to share in rituals of faith and legacy, and to experience unconditional love even in the hard times.

Every effort made and measure taken to provide all that and more for our families and guests can be done with a sense of gratitude and privilege. God has trusted each of us to cultivate beauty and grace where our loved ones reside. It's an honor whether we're living in a rented apartment, a temporary home, or a house where we've watched all our children grow up.

Feels Like Home

These are some of the delights and comforts that make any place, big or small, feel like home to me...

- Candles flickering
- Familiar music playing from the other room
- My four children and grandchildren discussing world events, stories, music, adventures
- Plenty of laughter
- The aroma of freshly baked cookies or buttered toast
- Various books in baskets and on shelves in every room
- Calligraphy of verses, quotes sprinkled around the house, framed paintings of English cottages and watercolors of the canal
- Thoughtful magazines, Bibles, art prints, family photos
- Strong cups of tea, cinnamon toast, lemon bread, scrambled cheese eggs
- Fresh bouquets from the market or wildflowers from the canal on display
- Musical instruments—guitar, piano, dulcimer—at the ready to be played
- A bench or chairs outside inviting us to take a load off and breathe in the breeze dancing on leaves, to smell pungent flowers growing in large tubs
- Art pencils and sketch books scattered for the creatives, sticker books for the grands
- A computer click-clicking as stories and books are conceived, podcasts recorded, music is scored, blogs are written
- In Oxford, we miss Darcy, our darling golden retriever, stealing goodies off our plates, tail wagging as she runs off. The tales we tell of her are a common thread in every home space.

What is on your list?

In my early years of parenting, I began to see my homes like gigantic treasure vaults to be filled with our own personal artifacts of life: dishes, artwork for the walls, books and magazines, music, movies, framed photographs to remind us of our personal connection to one another, and so much more. There are endless ways to create life, and we get to become the artists who leave our special imprint in and beyond our homes.

Doing this requires attention and commitment because as any parent knows, things don't always go as planned and the best intentions don't become realized actions in the blink of an eye. Early on, I learned life will always be complicated and plans are constantly interrupted. I understood that to create a sanctuary, I needed to be prepared with simple treasures and supplies.

As we add to our vault of riches, we are preparing our homes to be the welcoming, nurturing dwelling we want them to be. This is how the desire to create a loving space becomes a practice.

You may not have ever considered your advance planning and pursuit of extra touches to be the love traditions and practices that they are. We are curators of meaningful and memorable keepsakes—moments and objects—for our homes and our loved ones.

Some of the practices of preparation I've relied on are listed below. I hope you will find encouragement and be reminded of all you do to bring life to your home.

Cooking and Dining

- Shop the local markets for veggies and fruit, with a focus on fresh and organic.
- Freeze cookie dough balls, brownies, scones, bread in bags to pull out at a moment's notice; also make frozen meals such as casseroles, homemade soups, cooked chicken and fish to be heated for a cozy meal.
- Stock the cupboard with soups, canned goods, and basic baking ingredients.
- Keep ready-made cookies, biscuits, and jams on hand for last-minute visitors and teatime treats.
- Plan meals for family and guests ahead of time so you won't be overwhelmed when the crowds show up hungry.
- Invite guests and family—including the little ones—to help set tables, prepare centerpieces, and stir the food so everyone feels included.
- Be ready for impromptu meals and quick celebrations. Without a doubt, sharing thousands of meals as a family over the years has knit our hearts together as best friends.

Entertainment and Creative Play

- Collect board games, puzzles, lists of movies to stream, decks of cards, Legos, bubbles. Include favorites for all age groups.

- Plan activities and fun for family or guests such as treasure hunts, hikes, picnics, fireside chats, Easter egg hunts, and other seasonal traditions.

- Store child-friendly games in an accessible basket, cupboard, or drawer so they know they can go to it every time.

- If a house has room, fill a basket or bin with fun dress-up clothes, jewelry, and hats for planned or impromptu skit nights.

Art and Literature

- Collect books in many genres, filling shelves with picture books for littles, classic literature, adventure tales, hero stories, devotions, books about science and nature, biographies of artists and musicians, etc.

- Scour secondhand stores and antique markets for books with rousing stories, beautiful illustrations, and interesting subjects for children and all guests to read.

- Create cozy spaces throughout the home for reading with material within reach.

- Periodically change the art displayed in different rooms. I like to include art made by my children and the grands.

- Have a well-supplied arts and crafts closet, even if just with the basics.

- Create playlists of beautiful or interesting music for inspiring soundtracks for your life and for the special moments and memories created alongside guests.

- Have simple instruments around for spontaneous musical expression. Even a harmonica, kazoo, and a child's xylophone will make a happy noise.

Décor and Beauty

- Store holiday decorations in lidded plastic boxes for easy placement. In our home those are usually organized by Clay for Christmas, Easter, Thanksgiving, Fourth of July, Birthdays, etc.

- Create flower arrangements from simple, long-lasting flowers for scattering through the rooms or use baskets of pinecones, wreaths, or dry flowers to bring beauty.

- Frame photographs of special times and special places. Place some photos featuring the kids on the wall or atop tables at a height that suits their line of sight.

- Set out everyday decorations for beauty and to spark conversation. Recently I scattered bird and bunny figurines around my house. They bring delight to the little ones. Sometimes I make up a story based on the creature, or I invite the children to tell a tale of their own.

- Store candles to light at meals and to brighten nooks and set the mood for cozy comfort.

We are curators of meaningful and
memorable treasures—moments and objects—
for our homes and our loved ones.

Life is crafted little by little through the years. Every home can be a *beautiful* part of God's design, and you get to become the artist who crafts the life rhythms to ensure that love and faith are at the center and the sacred places and moments are honored over the years.

Each family will develop its own distinct way of living out the principles of wisdom

and delight that shape a home into a life-giving place. Because of this, each home will be uniquely suited to meet the needs of the children and parents who live there and of the guests who are invited to gather around the table or join in conversation.

We may call many places home during our lifetimes, yet each dwelling can be crafted with all the meaningful elements that matter to our families—a spirit of love, an invitation to belong, and beauty that is woven through each room.

I truly believe that the home we cultivate is one of the greatest works of our lives. We're creating training grounds for our children, shaping imaginations and values to be lived out in the world. We're creating a place where a child can be discipled and filled with love and care prior to growing up and heading to the battlefield of the world. The impact of an intentional place of welcome is eternal because the true transforming power of home goes heart, mind, and soul deep. People thrive when stability comes through belonging to a place and a people.

Our family is far from perfect. We have fusses, are all self-centered at times, have gone through the highs and lows of differing seasons of life. Broken hearts, disappointments, and failure have been born in the walls of our home. As a conductor of beauty and life in our home, I have had to learn how to strain forward toward wisdom, peacemaking, patience, and unconditional love.

As each of us grows toward maturity, we have emerged as unique individuals with

My people will live in peaceful dwelling places, in secure homes, in undisturbed places of rest.

ISAIAH 32:18 NIV

diverse personalities and preferences in life. I have sought to build a place that allows for individuality in the expression of life direction. And also, because of the attention to detail and design in our home, we all have a sense of belonging to one another, a sense of being a part of a community where we can find deep and abiding friendship and affirmation. We have learned how to become peacemakers to one another and how to live with affirmation of our differences.

> The impact of an intentional place of welcome is eternal because the true transforming power of home goes heart, mind, and soul deep. People thrive when stability comes through belonging to a place and a people.

*For this new morning
with its light,
Father, we thank Thee.
For rest and shelter
of the night,
Father, we thank Thee.
For health and food,
For love and friends,
For everything Thy
goodness sends,
Father in heaven,
we thank Thee.
Amen.*

RALPH WALDO EMERSON

Recently I asked one of my children if there was something special we could do to celebrate a coming birthday. I was thinking of a fun restaurant, an adventure to a nearby village, a dinner with friends. As my children are adults, I want to validate their freedom to do something with their friends.

"Mama, you want to know what I would love most? I want to come to your house, have our traditional cinnamon rolls, eat cheesy eggs together, sip tea, and be together as family to celebrate life as we did when we were little. That is my very favorite way to celebrate—being home together."

My heart could not have hoped for a better answer.

Better than gold is a peaceful home
Where all the fireside characters come,
The shrine of love, the heaven of life,
Hallowed by mother, or sister, or wife,
However humble the home may be,
Or tried with sorrow by heaven's decree,
The blessings that never were bought or sold,
And center there, are better than gold.

ABRAM J. RYAN

SIX

WE ALL FAIL,
WE ALL NEED GRACE

For through the grace given to me
I say to everyone among you not to think
more highly of himself than he ought to think;
but to think so as to have sound judgment,
as God has allotted to each a measure of faith.

ROMANS 12:3

Recently, after a book launch (I have survived many!), I entered a still-full schedule of doing podcast interviews, writing articles, speaking at conferences, and cooking meals, as well as hosting out-of-town guests. I found I was in a constant giving mode. As a seasoned woman, I can usually endure such busy times and insert enough rest and distraction to stay at least somewhat stable. As I returned to Oxford from my Colorado home, I held hope that my spirit would be restored once I was walking along meadow paths, gathering fresh flowers, and sitting on my small patio away from the bustle. Clay was joining me a few weeks later, so I wanted to use my solitary time to refill my cup and catch up on needed rest.

But soon I would be confronted with just how deeply weary I was.

Relief flooded me when I walked through the front door of my Oxford home. And I was glad to climb into bed that night in my little, cozy room. But the next morning I was disheartened. I'm sure the frustration of living out of

suitcases again and finding myself a little lonely and a bit lost in pending piles of responsibility left me fragile.

After a couple days, I decided to take myself out for a cup of tea down the street at one of my favorite cafés, which is my go-to when any source of life bubbles over and threatens to overwhelm. I had walked the steps and roads to this café many times. But I noticed this time, my gait was slow, my heart a bit heavy. Once settled in at a table, I sipped my tea and took a deep breath.

I happened to look up as one of my children walked into the café. When they waved to me, they had no idea the state of mind they would find me in.

"Hi, how are you?"

They greeted me with an innocent question, and I doubt either of us was prepared for my response. The storms of life were swirling inside me, and the pressure of my past weeks of stress was about to erupt. The too-long season of having no predictable order in my life, endless responsibilities, and the feeling that I was carrying it all by myself bubbled over. I began to spew and complain. My frustration wasn't just about this day; it seemed I had been storing up my feelings for quite a while. There were many layers of discouragement, disappointment, anger, and frustration rising to the surface.

As my overwhelm flowed, I could see I was causing great stress for my child. I had made a commitment to restrain my "dumping" to a minimum. Surprise and stress were showing all over their face—and they had not done anything wrong. If only I could take back my words.

Of course, as soon as I stopped ranting, I was appalled at myself. *What good mother loses control like that and pours potential guilt and disappointment all over an unsuspecting*

*Take my yoke upon
you and learn from me,
for I am gentle and
humble in heart,
and you will find
rest for your souls.*

MATTHEW 11:29 NIV

child when the cause for the frustration has nothing to do with them? What damage had I done?

Luckily, my beloved, who had been totally unprepared for my blast, quietly said, "Are you feeling a little bit exhausted from the international flight? The book launch? Being alone the past few days? Maybe you just need to have a good night sleep and then look at your world all over again."

Has one of your adult children ever been the adult who counseled you? Does anyone else ever feel this shameful regret? After all, I am a fairly mature believer. I write about faith, I love my children, and I am grateful for my husband. But my life is far from perfect and comes with its own set of stresses. So what is it that comes over me at these times?

Then inadequacy shook its finger at my heart, and voices whispered to me in my failure, "Maybe you should quit writing and speaking."

My sweet one continued, "Did you know that Andrew Peterson is in town? He's singing at a concert tonight. I bet if you went with me you would really enjoy it and be encouraged."

Andrew has been a friend for many years, and our family has attended his conferences and we've been engaged together in ministry. The evening show was a welcome offer. He was only in Oxford a couple of times a year, and gratefully I had not missed the yearly event.

After some soulful, sympathetic songs, Andrew began to sing a familiar favorite, "Be Kind to Yourself." This song had been written for his children to remind them that all of us fail, all of us are self-critical, and all of us need to lean into the generous, endless healing grace of our compassionate heavenly Father.

Every song, every lyric seemed as though it were written just for me.

Sally, be kind to yourself, it seemed as though God was whispering to me.

Sometimes I punish myself when I blow it, as though I am above making mistakes and am shocked at my failure. I hate to hurt the feelings of my family or friends or dump my fraught emotions on them. Yet I know most of us blow it in some way almost every day. We are selfish at heart, limited in virtue, and in need of forgiveness—but mostly we need the grace of living beyond our guilt.

Our Shortcomings, His Strength

Each of us is tempted at times to feel the kind of pride that pretends we are better than others. However, Jesus was so very clear about our nature and propensity to fall short in

Chocolate
Fudge

every ideal possible. John wrote, "If we say that we have no sin, we are deceiving ourselves" (1 John 1:8).

Jesus does not judge me by my fleshly frailty but by my heart of love for Him, my utter dependence on His grace, and my heart of gratitude for His enduring patience.

> # We are selfish at heart, limited in virtue, and in need of forgiveness— but mostly we need the grace of living beyond our guilt.

If you have blown it and feel like a failure, walk in His wonderful grace today, even in the midst of your shortcomings. Remember, you are defined by *His* strength and provision, not your own limitations. This is why you need a Savior. He forgets our sin, but we remember His grace and humbly walk each day with Him.

When I got home, I opened my Bible and was deeply comforted and began to be restored:

Love covers a multitude of sins.
1 PETER 4:8

It was for freedom that Christ set us free; therefore keep standing firm and do not be subject again to a yoke of slavery.
GALATIANS 5:1

For I am convinced that neither death, nor life, nor angels, nor principalities, nor things present, nor things to come, nor powers, nor height, nor depth, nor

*any other created thing will be able to separate us
from the love of God that is in Christ Jesus our Lord.*

ROMANS 8:38-39

*My grace is sufficient for you, for power
is perfected in weakness.*

2 CORINTHIANS 12:9

*Do you think lightly of the riches of His kindness
and restraint and patience, not knowing that the
kindness of God leads you to repentance?*

ROMANS 2:4

Over the years I have learned that no one else can take responsibility for my life, my feelings, or my pressure. Yet God is constantly with me, a beloved companion ready to show me His understanding, His patience, His kindness.

*Be completely
humble and gentle;
be patient, bearing with
one another in love.*

EPHESIANS 4:2 NIV

I have also realized, though, that to stay more filled up, more able to face the stresses, I have to find ways that restore me on a regular basis so that I can mount up over the pressures.

Daily I look for ways to develop peace and quiet in my heart amidst the constant demands of life and the ever-present people who live with me. The canal pathway near my home is a favorite place I walk to restore this peace of heart from which I respond to others. It is beautiful, calming, a natural haven. I also spend time immersed in literature and books of faith and knowledge to nurture my mind and spirit. Background music always wafts through my rooms

to soothe me. Feeding my curiosity and hunger for wisdom through regular, scheduled meetings with close friends satisfies my soul and brings such deep calm and comfort.

<blockquote>
God is constantly with me, a beloved companion ready to show me His understanding, His patience, His kindness.
</blockquote>

Acknowledging and seeing my own immature tendencies and failures has brought about a deep beauty and fruit in my life. The older I am, the more I see my inadequacies, selfishness, and propensity to behave in an immature way. This realization has led me to have more mercy, compassion, and patience with others, especially my children. My ability to extend sympathy instead of criticism in my responses has grown.

For it is by grace you have been saved, through faith—and this is not from yourselves, it is the gift of God—not by works, so that no one can boast.

EPHESIANS 2:8-9 NIV

Longing for Gentleness

Truly seeing your weaknesses and failings will change your heart and from there, change your behavior toward others. When you know how much you long for someone to be patient with you and experience how soothing and heart-opening it is when others are kind and forgiving, it will change your attitude and behavior toward your children. Grace makes way for grace.

A young mom sat across the table from me at a café recently. A steaming coffee in hand, head bowed. "I just don't know what to do," she said. "My daughter won't obey me. Her toys are always spread throughout the house, even though I tell her to clean them up. She won't go to bed when I tell her it's time. And every time she refuses to obey, I get more and more angry. There was a lot of yelling in my house when I was little, and I hated it. But now…" She shook her head, a tear slipping down her cheek. "I'm doing the exact same thing I hated so much from my parents—yelling! And I can't figure out how to stop. I'm an awful mom! And the guilt is overwhelming. Maybe I shouldn't have had children."

I shook my head and reached my hand across the table to cover hers. "No. That's just not true," I reassured her. "I know what it's like to lose your temper. All women get frustrated and lose their patience from time to time. No one likes out of control anger or yelling—parents or children. But being frustrated at these aspects of life is normal. It doesn't mean you are a failure."

She nodded, trying to soak in the moment of being seen and accepted.

I continued, wanting to be sure she felt God's love and not just my own. "The more you can mother from rest, peace, and a heart that has experienced God's grace and unconditional love, the less you will feel defeated and frustrated, and the more your child will learn how to respond to you. Cherish and practice gentleness, patience, mercy."

I wish someone had told me when I was younger how often I'd fail, be tempted to feel guilty, have the feeling that it was all up to me—and how useless that feeling would be to me long-term and to those I was loving and serving.

Before I became a wife or parent, I assumed I would be able to be mature, healthy, loving, and successful in these relationships all the time. Conflict in my own heart and life, and the stress of living with so many needs and so many constant demands, showed me my selfishness—or at least my exhaustion and emptiness.

Always to be gentle toward everyone.

TITUS 3:2 NIV

I longed for mercy, but especially for gentleness. I wanted to be understood—that I had a heart to be good at these relationships but *sometimes I just couldn't*—but my own selfishness got in the way. I meant to be patient, giving, loving, but I had my limits. As an idealist with a "feeler" heart, I wanted compassion and sympathy, but especially a gentle response—not anger and condemnation.

And so did my friends, children, and husband. The people who come to me desire respect, acceptance, and gentleness in handling them when they are imperfect or irritate me. And it was through my different children, and the demands of everyday life, that I learned the need for gentleness, and that I, too, craved another chance—again.

At what point does a woman find the ability to be gentle, to show mercy, understanding, compassion?

When she understands that her heart is immature, prone to making bad choices, limited in patience, and just beginning to comprehend what love requires. She acknowledges that she herself is fragile; she learns how to extend the grace she wishes to receive to others she loves, because they, too, are fragile and want gentleness and mercy.

If a woman understands that others, like her, are going to make mistakes, have accidents, show the dark heart of criticism and pettiness, she will not condemn them harshly for behaving in the same way she does. Instead, from a heart that knows she does not deserve the grace and love of Jesus, but receives it nonetheless, she will extend her patience, mercy, and gentleness to others to show them the real heart of Jesus.

She will still teach, train, correct as Jesus did, knowing that compassion comes from a humbled heart and mercy overflows from a heart that recognizes the need for grace and forgiveness. Mercy is a response of grace to someone who deserves condemnation but is in need of love and grace.

I used to think that my children would judge me or be disappointed in me if I was not perfect in my love for them. I held myself to a standard of performance, not grace, and judged my worth by how well I thought I was doing. But the pressure to perform well was high, and I could never seem to quite live up to it.

I remember a late afternoon when one of my daughters had been really frustrated and out of sorts with a close friend. Guilt followed.

"How about a walk in the University Parks and then a flat white?" I suggested. It was where we often strolled together, to share thoughts and secrets amongst the benches and beauty of the wildness. I put my arm around her and said, "You are one of the loveliest people I know. You are gentle, kind, thoughtful—but you will never be perfect, just as I will never be."

All my experience of the world teaches me that in ninety-nine cases out of a hundred, the safe and just side of a question is the generous and merciful side.

ANNA JAMESON

She relaxed as we strolled along. The next words I spoke to her anxious heart are also for you, my friend. They are for me too. We need reminders that we are always under God's grace and love, even when—particularly when—we are lamenting our flaws, our failings. "We are human beings with needs, emotions, desires, personality. We learn little by little to grow stronger so that we might learn how to merge our real selves with the reality of the relationships in which we find ourselves. Maturity is a long process. It is a practice of learning not to react in an unloving way. You will never, ever be perfect, my precious, but I love who you are right now in the process. And God loves you so dearly and wants you to know His mercy and understanding of how you feel."

"Mama, I feel so understood."

The peace of the gentle breeze in the trees seemed to match the grace that both of us breathed in through our quiet moments there in our sanctuary of His making.

The next time you struggle, the next time you make a mistake or are dwelling on your flaws, pause and breathe in the grace of God. He is your beloved companion.

In you, Father all-mighty, we have
our preservation and our bliss.
In you, Christ, we have our
restoring and our saving.
You are our mother, brother, and savior.
In you, our Lord the Holy Spirit, is
marvelous and plenteous grace.
You are our clothing; for love you
wrap us and embrace us.
You are our maker, our lover, our keeper.
Teach us to believe that by your
grace all shall be well,
and all shall be well,
and all manner of things shall be well.
Amen.

JULIAN OF NORWICH

Every day is a fresh beginning,
Every morn in the world made new,
You who are weary of sorrow and sinning,
Here is a beautiful hope for you,—
A hope for me and a hope for you...

Every day is a fresh beginning;
Listen, my soul, to the glad refrain,
And spite of old sorrow and older sinning,
And puzzles forecasted and possible pain,
Take heart with the day, and begin again.

SUSAN COOLIDGE

SEVEN

SURPRISED BY KINDNESS

Do not neglect to show hospitality to strangers,
for thereby some have entertained angels unawares.

HEBREWS 13:2 ESV

Christmas in the Clarkson home is a warm celebration filled with traditions, feasting of all sorts, crowds of people stuffed into small rooms, music, lights, and noise. My smaller Oxford home found all of us a little closer in proximity than normal this Christmas Day, as well as more aware of the chatter and noise in every room. We had adults, grandchildren, toys at every twist and turn.

After a morning of unwrapping gifts, eating a homemade breakfast, and sipping tea, everyone found a comfy spot in the house to catch a breath and talk some more. My introverted son, Joel, tapped me on the shoulder and whispered, "Would you want to go on a short walk with me to the canal and get away from the entourage for a few minutes? It might be nice to have a few moments of peace and quiet." He sheepishly smiled with eyes expressing a need to escape for a brief time.

When one of my adult children wants time with me alone, I make room for their request. It feels like such an honor to be able to count them as my best friends, even now that they are grown. So Joel and I slipped out unnoticed, and began to meander in the cold, crisp winter air.

Our home backed up to an Oxford canal where boats glide by or are moored for the night. Daily we walked the beautiful pathway by old Victorian homes and tall apartment buildings separated by bridges here and there that fed into

*Happy is the house
that shelters a friend.*

RALPH WALDO EMERSON

the villages nearby. Oxford canals are a 78-mile waterway that starts by the River Thames and runs mostly through tranquil, rolling countryside. Once a transport route for commercial boats filled with coal and other goods, the canals served the long, narrow boats carrying their cargo from one town to the other. Most canals were built over a couple of hundred years ago, starting in 1769. Currently long boats have been turned into houseboats or vacation boats occupying the waterways.

The walking paths are filled with natural growth of trees, flowers, swans, ducks, cranes, and other small wildlife scattered here and there. This had become one of our favorite walking paths for our daily pleasure, a perfect escape for introverts' getaways.

As it was Christmas Day, the pathways were empty, with families gathered in their various homes. This made for a delightful opportunity to catch up as friends. After a leisurely walk, Joel and I found an old, beaten-up bench tucked into the thick woods where we decided to sit and enjoy the quiet and beauty surrounding us.

A lovely painted boat was moored right in front of us. As we chatted and rested a few minutes, the door of the boat suddenly opened. A lovely, well-dressed white-headed woman appeared carrying an ornate silver tray holding two crystal glasses filled with sherry.

"You looked like you might need a little warming up out here all alone in the woods. We hoped you were not having a lonely Christmas." Hardly! "My husband and I thought we might share a drink with you and wish you well on this Christmas Day. Would you accept our wish for you for a bit of Christmas cheer?"

Delighted by her gracious offering, we took the sparkling glasses and gratefully sipped with a smile and with spirits warmed by the gesture.

"We will leave you to your peace," she said as she smiled and she and her husband disappeared into the depths of their boat. It was as though a wood fairy had appeared from nowhere

to wish us well in this stolen moment on this gorgeous winter's day. We sipped slowly, breathed in their gracious, hospitable words and drink, and felt as though we had been kissed by God. A secret moment shared with kind people was just what we needed, even though we had not realized it.

Before we ever appeared at the mooring of their boat, these dear people had already made a heartfelt decision to be hospitable to many in their lives. One who has determined to be a hostess of grace anticipates emotional, physical, and spiritual needs and then ponders how to extend hospitality freely and generously as opportunities present themselves. We called her our Christmas angel of kindness, who filled our hearts with merriness and joy.

A Willing Heart

In a time when pristine images come at us nonstop from Instagram, home decor magazines, and social media posts, it is easy to become inundated with ideas for a perfectly decked-out home as the place where elaborate parties take place in the name of hospitality.

The King will reply, "Truly I tell you, whatever you did for one of the least of these brothers and sisters of mine, you did for me."

MATTHEW 25:40 NIV

Yet hospitality is not necessarily fancy or elaborate but is always the selfless consideration of how to meet the needs of another person. A life well lived is one in which hospitality and kindness (the consideration of someone else's needs) is a natural habit of expressing the welcome, love, and grace of God in a practical way.

From the very beginning, hospitality was an expected act of worship to God. God first extended hospitality to Adam and Eve when He created a world full of beauty, food, a place to satisfy their basic needs as well as their pleasure. Hospitality is an intrinsic expression of the nature of God. Throughout the Bible, God gives us many stories of gracious sharing. Rahab risked her life and protected the spies in her home. Abraham saw three tired strangers and invited them to sit in the shade of a tree while he prepared a meal for them. During a devastating drought, a widow sacrificed her limited supplies and made bread for Elijah. As Elijah said would happen, God blessed her offering: her jar of flour and a jug of olive oil remained replenished until rains returned to the land. Jesus lovingly prepared a holy time for His last evening with His beloved disciples by choosing a quiet room, away from the noisy crowds. Food was carefully cooked and laid out for them. Each man was served by having his dusty, dirty feet washed by the gentle hands of their Master.

Hospitality starts with a heart willing to serve and give generously. Our hearts must practice attitudes of generosity—we must perceive ourselves as agents of kindness before we even meet someone. We give because He gives to us. And meeting the needs of others opens their hearts to our messages of God's love and grace.

A life well lived is one in which hospitality is
a natural habit of expressing the welcome,
love, and grace of God in a practical way.

To go through life looking for ways to meet the needs of others is a reflection of a person who is sensitive to the direction of the Holy Spirit, whose value it is to meet the needs of others.

Time after time, as both a giver and a recipient, I have experienced the impact a simple gesture of kindness and hospitality makes. During the late 1970s, I was attending language school in Austria. I found my way around this strange city, and even learned how to buy groceries with my very limited German, but I longed for a personal connection. I wished for someone to talk to who understood the foreignness of being in a country where few people fluently spoke my native language.

One day a young woman, also new to the country, said to me the dearest words I had heard in months: "Come in and sit for a while and let's be friends." The invitation and the time together was so meaningful to me, I can still recall what she served that night: meatloaf, cottage cheese, and steamed broccoli. Not fancy, but so familiar and comforting. I remember it as one of the best meals of my life because it was served with such kindness and love. She extended the hospitality of Jesus to me, and it warmed me to my tippy-toes.

True hospitality consists of giving the best of yourself to your guests.

ELEANOR ROOSEVELT

This kind of heart hospitality is the heart of my own home. I want to extend that feeling of being invited in, welcomed, and understood to my children as well as friends who come to spend time with us.

Hospitality comes from the same root word as *hospital, hospice,* and *hotel.* Behind the words is the idea that hospitality seeks to provide for, protect, and care for the person who dwells in or visits your home.

One who is hospitable gathers resources so they may be ready to meet the needs of others. We have always had guest rooms available for those who would stay in our home, even if it meant giving up our own bedrooms. Having clean sheets, comfy bed covers, bottles of water on the bedside table, nuts and fruit, some dark chocolate, and a cupboard or freezer full of easily fixable meals is a part of our whole home plan to be ready to invite others who need shelter in our place.

Hospitality need not be complicated or expensive. We can create hospitable moments as my wood fairy did that day on the canal when we are emotionally prepared to pause the busyness of our lives to extend kindness and help to those who come across our path. Readiness to help is the foundation of being willing to interrupt our own schedules to meet the felt and real needs of others.

To go through life looking for ways to meet the needs of others is a reflection of a person who is sensitive to the direction of the Holy Spirit.

Humble Hospitality

When living in Oxford, we were surrounded by people from different countries, with differing languages and a wide variety of needs. Because they were away from their homeland, they longed for friendship, help, and fellowship. I stretched even more into the direction of a hospitable life than I had sought to cultivate before because needs were so obvious. The focus on how to love and serve people in my life practically through food and physical and emotional care provided me with new goals in setting up my home to meet needs.

This desire required even more creativity than usual when the two years of Covid offered special challenges when extending hospitality. Just after we moved into our home in Oxford, Covid hit the UK and we were prohibited from having more than four people in our homes. The people allowed to be with us in our home were considered those who were in our bubble.

As we were just getting used to these new rules, I decided I would host a Bible study outside in the open garden, where being together would be both safe and allowed.

I wanted to meet some women in the area, so I literally put out an announcement on social media asking if anyone wanted to get together once a week for fellowship and a book study. To my surprise, I received 15 positive responses to my invitation. I was excited and eager to prepare for these new friends. Clay and I bought folding chairs to accommodate our guests out of doors and the new group began to meet.

It wasn't long before rainy nights threatened to disrupt our gatherings. I was determined not to let the weather stop what was becoming an important part of everyone's week. It dawned on me that there was a logical solution between hosting inside and outside—our garage. We did not own a car, so our garage was filled with boxes, suitcases, a few tools, and garden rakes. We scooted all our various boxes and goods to the sides of our garage, placed chairs in a circle, and opened the garage door so fresh air could circulate.

I brought out to the garage a small, old teacart on wheels I had purchased at an open-air market. I set out the prepared tea, coffee, and baked goods along with several candles to light up our room and to provide ambience on this old cart. Nothing fancy, but a gracious welcome extended to each woman who came.

Even when we had to bundle up to ease the winter chill, women delighted in our makeshift outdoor room. This became the place where friendships were forged, women were encouraged, and life flowed. Over time, even their children became friends as they began to get together outside the meeting times. Shared meals were occasionally a part of the gatherings. And new friends were invited over time as people moved in and out of Oxford. This is the third year we have met, and now the friendships are deepening. Together, we have welcomed the births of babies, sent

friends back to their home countries with prayers and celebrations, and mourned with those whose struggles threatened to overwhelm.

Eventually a friend from London came every week to help me set up, and to provide flowers, cakes, and encouragement. She stayed in our guest room, and we dubbed the room "Jacqui's room" because of her regular visits.

Our need for friendship and fellowship during this isolated time meant we did not care about the rough walls, the crowded room, the paint cans stacked in the corners. But we did care that we could meet as friends and not feel so alone. As the pandemic rules eased, we met inside the house. But our gathering was made sweeter and stronger because of its humble beginnings. Our connection was not based on fancy but on faithfulness. The bond created was built on love given, truth taught, encouragement felt, and of course, stomachs and hearts fed.

Whether it is a child, a stranger, a relative, or a neighbor, we have found that a sincere welcome and a simple treat to nourish or delight another opens hearts to the love of God. Even as God is at the center of our own invitation to experience His pleasure, kindness, and provision, there must be a person willing to host, ready to reach out, practiced at meeting real needs. A well-lived life naturally and beautifully includes hospitality, and through this commitment, friendships will be cultivated and stories told of angels entertained. Thoughtfulness and kindness win the day.

Lord of all pots and pans and things,
since I've no time to be a great saint
by doing lovely things,
or watching late with Thee,
or dreaming in the dawn light,
or storming heaven's gates,
make me a saint by getting meals,
and washing up the plates...
Warm all the kitchen with Thy love,
and light it with Thy peace;
forgive me all my worrying,
and make my grumbling cease.
Thou who didst love to give men food,
in room, or by the sea,
accept the service that I do,
I do it unto Thee.
Amen.

KLARA MUNKRES

Even as God is at the center of our own invitation to experience His pleasure and provision, there must be a person willing to host, ready to reach out, practiced at meeting real needs.

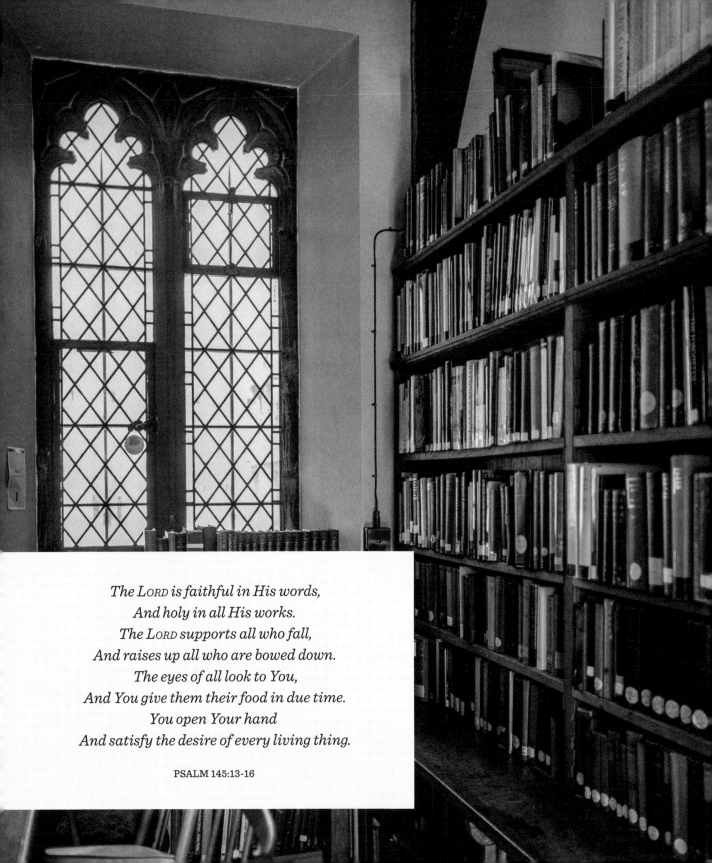

The LORD is faithful in His words,
And holy in all His works.
The LORD supports all who fall,
And raises up all who are bowed down.
The eyes of all look to You,
And You give them their food in due time.
You open Your hand
And satisfy the desire of every living thing.

PSALM 145:13-16

EIGHT

THE TWO BECOME ONE

"For this reason a man shall leave his father and mother and
be joined to his wife, and the two shall become one flesh";
so then they are no longer two, but one flesh. Therefore
what God has joined together, let not man separate.

MARK 10:7-9 NKJV

A few years ago, one of my grown children asked to visit. So with steeped tea, lit candles, music playing, chocolate chip cookies baked, and a cup ready to be filled, I set up our kitchen for a heart-to-heart. We settled in, chatted for a bit. It wasn't long before the reason for the meeting came out.

"Mama, what do you wish you had known about marriage when you first started out? Do all marriages have to be hard?"

As it happened, several of our family friends and some members in my mentoring group had recently found themselves embroiled in marital difficulties and had separated from their spouses. I saw in the eyes of this child a deeply sincere desire to cultivate a marriage with the hopes that it would be good, foundationally affirming, with the possibility of flourishing. Witnessing the division of friends who divorced, or separated, or experienced years of pain in a broken relationship had created a small tinge of fear.

I prayed for wisdom to give a satisfying and honest answer that did not ignore the challenges that come from two sinful people living together through all the stresses and difficulties of life. More than anything, I wanted to offer true answers that would give insight for differing seasons, reasons to hold fast, and a model for how to imagine the journey at each season.

Dancing Partners Through Thick or Thin

As I considered the weight of the question my adult child posed to me that day and how I could best encourage them, a memory of a family tradition came to mind. Gathering around the television every four years to watch the Olympics was a must in our family. Of particular interest were the ice-skating competitions. We were mesmerized by the pairs events and the synchronized beauty of perfect unity, twirls, and extraordinary jumps.

Often, in interviews after performances, the skaters shared tales of difficulty, injuries, setbacks, and discouragement along the journey. Yet what we would see was the result of years of practice, diligence, knowing their partner well, creativity, skill, perseverance, the secrets to a beautiful dance. The performing couples would say the key to winning was becoming intuitive to their partner's personality and the ways they expressed dynamic motion, to anticipate the various moves of the dance as an elegant picture of unity learned over years of performing together.

To become such partners, there had to be years of working together, building trust, seeking unity within the routine, understanding the other person's movements and actions. Falls and mishaps, bruises and bumps were an understood and anticipated part of the journey. Times of discouragement and feelings of wanting to quit were some of the elements that were in the background of a stellar performance. But to become champions, both had to keep getting up after a fall, refining the problematic movement that caused them to fall in the first place, pushing through to commence with a sublime dance of grace, beauty, and skill, and cultivating passion for expression of their skill. In short, such an accomplishment required discipline, diligence, patience, commitment, and a vision for what they could accomplish together.

Two are better than one, because they have a good return for their labor: If either of them falls down, one can help the other up.

ECCLESIASTES 4:9-10 NIV

What a beautiful metaphor for marriage—a dance of love. Always learning, growing stronger, practicing wisdom, honoring the potential and ways of the other, creating beauty, drawing closer as partners, and determining to "get up" again and again after a relational fall.

I shared this example with my child who desired reassurance and hope about marriage. I wanted them to know a lasting, happy union was indeed possible and that it could be beautiful, that God created marriage to be a deep fulfillment and satisfaction in life. And that marriage is a long dance of life made up of twists and turns, resulting in a beauty and unity that shows the world the intrigue, mystery, elegance, and value of the most

Nothing is sweeter than love, nothing stronger, nothing loftier, nothing broader, nothing pleasanter, nothing fuller or better in heaven nor on earth, for love was born of God and cannot rest save in God above all created things.

THOMAS À KEMPIS

sacred trust. Though passion might be strong in the beginning, and disappointments found along the way, the ones who persevere in the life partnership will find it one of the most meaningful legacies of life.

As someone who has been married for more than 42 years, I have had plenty of time to reflect on what it takes to strengthen and protect a marriage. I understand there are seasons of joy and seasons of deep struggle, and the honorable holding of the marital sacred trust is the work of a lifetime. When a couple finds grace to create a precious trust and can nurture that trust to cause the relationship to flourish, a story of strength, companionship, and truth unfolds—a story that offers hope to others that their marriage can endure and thrive. Our world is in great need of seeing the reality of a marriage through a well-told story of a flourishing, lifelong partnership.

Marriage is a long dance of life made up of twists and turns, resulting in a beauty and unity that shows the world the intrigue, mystery, elegance, and value of the most sacred trust.

Rising Above a Fallen Relationship

All relationships are fraught with difficulties. The demands of parenting, marriage, and friendship are challenging. One of the most consistent ways we observe the fallenness of humans is in our inability to love one another, to get along, to have peace and understanding. Our sin nature causes us to see the world and people from our own perspective, which means we justify our attitudes and behaviors because we suppose we are right, even when we are imperfect.

The hurt, harm, and upheaval that emerge because of the sinful self lens are witnessed in war, marriage, parenting, friendship, work. One of the realities of this fallen relationship principle is that no matter how earnestly we try, no matter how kind and selfless we think we are being, we cannot please all people. And we certainly cannot please our main person and our family members all of the time.

The happiness of married life depends upon making small sacrifices with readiness and cheerfulness.

JOHN SELDON

Throughout much of history, mothers and fathers lived near their parents, aunts, grandparents, cousins; there was help, companionship, a devoted community to share the load. But now we exist in a culture where people are most likely to be alone in the town in which they live without the help of family or community. They brave the demands and stresses of living (finances, job security, illness, childcare) alone. And because most don't even know they were created to have these support systems, they have become accustomed to believing all of their needs and desires should be met by their spouse. This expectation places an overwhelming burden on the marriage. The result is often more criticism, more disappointment, and plenty of frustration.

This is why we need to understand the principle of unconditional love. It is natural to disdain or criticize people; it is supernatural to love, to forgive, to be patient. We can rise above the reality of fallen relationships. Instead of reciprocating a person's indifference or lack of grace, we can love them because we have the mercy, strength, and help of the Holy Spirit. To love in spite of others' flaws is truly a remarkable act of believers who allow the Holy Spirit to love others through us no matter how they have offended or disappointed us.

The Holy Spirit teaches us to practice gracious responses, to speak with a gentle voice, to heal broken relationships, to move forward in unconditional love. Jesus is our model for all relationships. We will never be perfect in love, but we practice love as a service of worship to God because He tells us to, because He loves us even though we do not deserve it.

This is why we need to understand the principle of unconditional love. It is natural to disdain or criticize people; it is supernatural to love, to forgive, to be patient.

Clay and I are no exception as a couple. We both had to face being imperfect and partnering with another imperfect human. Differing personalities created conflicting choices for some of the values we would establish for our family. Because we were both unseasoned and young, we had to work together to overcome the misunderstandings and miscommunications that arose. We had to learn to serve one another, to do what was best for our family without undue regard to our own personal preferences. We had to learn to give up the demand to "be right."

At some point, we had to acknowledge that both of us were flawed, that we would never be perfect or able to change in some areas. We had to seek out support systems rather than wrongly expect or demand the other person to be *all things* in *all situations.* Choosing not to criticize one another for not being perfectly able to meet needs was a part of bringing peace and freedom to our relationship so that neither of us feared one more critical attitude toward our fragility of imperfection.

Coming together is a beginning; keeping together is progress; working together is success.

HENRY FORD

Of course we needed to cultivate companionship and pleasure that complemented our unique partnership and desires. But ultimately, it was our undaunted commitment to stay faithful to the vows we had given before God that kept us moving forward. We both slowly moved from petty arguments and shallow criticism to giving grace, making peace, asking for forgiveness. Our longing for harmony was greater than our desire to have our own way. Selfishness and throwing out words of anger and engaging in petty quarrels always made us feel worse than if we had just chosen to overlook one another's differences.

The love and passion and even conflict of our early marriage grew over time into a deeper, more mature love with great value. Having experienced three miscarriages and the loss of those babies meant there was someone else who had borne the grief with me in an intimate way—it was his loss of a child as well. When we were blessed to enter parenthood, we then faced all that was required in that endeavor together. We grew and learned together through the years of little sleep; training our children toward maturity; keeping them fed, clothed, and flourishing through every stage and age; learning to cultivate unconditional love and peacemaking as a standard of our values.

Watching our children become strong, seek to know and serve God, and wrestle to find their way in adult life became a beautiful, mutual work that helped to forge our unity as a couple. Through the decades, we parented together with a mutual plan and application of the values, virtues, and traditions we crafted.

Our vision created our lifelong faithfulness.

Shared Highs, Shared Lows

Entering into the high-stakes relationship of marriage requires a vision that is strong enough to carry you through every season a life might hold. Perseverance in times when discouragement whispers "quit" is also a measure of the ultimate story. Forgiveness for mishaps and acceptance of the reality of flaws in both partners has to be a foundational understanding for both. Grace exercised many times in many ways strengthens the muscle of love.

At this stage of my life, I can look back and see the preciousness of the dance Clay and I have choreographed with our lives, choices, and commitments. It has given both of us great joy and deep satisfaction. We have only felt this sweet reward because we determined we would endure together with a focus on growing in the direction of unity, humility, sacrifice, and unconditional love.

As we waltzed through the steps and turns of our own life routine, we grew ever closer in moving to the rhythm of each other in partnership. We learned to celebrate to our unique beat of life while intuiting one another's movement because of much practice over a lifetime.

A couple of years ago, I discovered I needed a hip replacement. I found myself helplessly sitting on our living room couch, unable to move after surgery, and my husband came in

Grow old along with me!
The best is yet to be,
The last of life, for which
the first was made:
Our times are in His hand
Who saith, "A whole
I planned,
Youth shows but half;
trust God: see all,
nor be afraid!"

ROBERT BROWNING

*A good marriage is
one which allows for
change and growth
in the individuals
and in the way they
express their love.*

PEARL S. BUCK

every day and put socks on my feet to keep them warm. He brought me a hot cup of tea, made breakfast, and made sure I had reading material and my little music speaker. He anticipated my needs and helped me without me even asking.

It dawned on me anew that the gift of having a partner with whom to share all the joys and sorrows of life, the burdens and the grace, is a beautiful dance. Our dance was uniquely suited to our individual story. Just as each of the couples in the ice-skating competition chose their own music and in a certain genre, melodies put to their own creative choice of moves and steps, so each of us has agency and freedom to craft the details of our own story to suit our personal decisions and desires. No two marriages are alike. And there is no list of rules that can cover every potential conflict. Only a commitment to faith, love, and grace will energize the relationship.

When we realize we are partnered to honor the other's strengths, forgive the missteps, twirl in the times of delight, and lift up the other when one falls, we are able to make our way through the many days and dance steps toward a deep and loving relationship. We are able to flourish through thick and thin as partners.

*O Divine Master,
grant that I may not
so much seek to be
consoled as to console;
to be understood as
to understand;
to be loved as to love;
for it is in giving
that we receive,
it is in pardoning that
we are pardoned,
and it is in dying that we
are born to eternal life.
Amen.*

ST. FRANCIS OF ASSISI

My dance with Clay has been complex and complicated. We lived to our own unique music. And so it is with each marriage, a unique portrayal of the personalities and stories merging together into a graceful, orchestrated dance with individual twists and turns. Managing the steps in harmony with one another took practice as well as diligence to keep learning and living into the partnership we held as sacred. Having someone share the workload and the pleasures of life knitted our hearts together over years.

Our unique and beautiful dance gained more value with each year's mutually shared life events and experiences. And now, as I move into my last decades, sympathy, help, kindness,

and consideration mean more to me than I ever knew they would. Love is a legacy over a lifetime that creates a beautiful story worth remembering for generations to come.

To grow strong in marriage takes a mutual commitment by both partners to keep going, to keep learning, to keep loving, to stay faithful through all the seasons. How wise God was to provide such a design of two persons working out their own story by faith and with love. The needful help of a partner through the seasons means we can face the challenges of our lives with the help, love, and support of another.

What greater thing is there for two human souls than to feel that they are joined for life—to strengthen each other in all labor, to rest on each other in all sorrow, to minister to each other in all pain, to be one with each other in silent, unspeakable memories at the moment of the last parting.

GEORGE ELIOT

NINE

LOVE ONE ANOTHER

So now faith, hope, and love abide, these
three; but the greatest of these is love.

1 CORINTHIANS 13:13 ESV

One Sunday afternoon nature invited all of Oxford to its outdoor playground. After a very long stretch of dark, cold, and rainy days, the sun was shining, the temperature was at least moderate, and I think literally everyone and their dog was outside! And most of them seemed to be wandering the street I needed to navigate to meet my friend.

A glance at my watch confirmed I was running late. As I hurried along the crowded and cobbled streets, I reminded myself that my dear friend would certainly wait for me. I took a deep breath and slowed slightly to avoid tripping over the sidewalk sign for a restaurant. Because I don't have a car, walking is my most common mode of travel, and as I was prone to falling on hurried occasions, I was constantly talking to myself about being careful.

I looked ahead in time to see my friend biking quickly toward me. I laughed to myself. Ah, so we were both late and trying to maneuver around the droves of sunseekers. After she found a spot for her bike, we exchanged a warm hug and greeting and strolled together to our destination—an outdoor coffee café that we hoped would have a table despite the crowds. As I had been on a speaking tour for a month, I had missed my sweet, gentle friend and looked so forward to being together.

We arrived to the café and stood beneath its awning where we both paused, happily anticipating which pastry we might pair with our coffee that morning.

*Deepen your love
in me, O Lord...
Let my soul spend
itself in your praise,
rejoicing for love.
Let me love you more
than myself, and myself
only for your sake.
Let me love others, as your
law commands. Amen.*

THÉRÈSE OF LISIEUX

As we were about to go in, a lovely young woman crossed our path. She had the most beautiful black hair piled high on her head in braids. Without thinking much, I said to her, "Your hair is absolutely gorgeous!" That was all I said. I am used to being surrounded by many students. Being friendly and getting to know them is just a part of my daily life. Their presence draws me to, in some small way, add grace to their day.

The young woman's face came alive. "Oh, do you think so? Thank you so much. I am just visiting here in Oxford and hoping to attend to study for my master's degree."

"How wonderful!" I said.

She then proceeded to chat with us as though she had been waiting all day for someone to talk to her. "I come from a small town in Africa. It has been my dream for my whole life to study at Oxford. I am here for a visit. I was hoping to talk to someone about what it is like to live here. I haven't found anyone all day who had the time to talk with me."

And so my friend and I began to tell her all about the possibilities of living here and answering her questions. She was so eager to talk to us, total strangers. "You know, I teach a Bible study here for students working on their graduate degrees. There are women from all over the world, differing ages, studying a variety of subjects. You are welcome to join us," I said as we reached for the door.

"You are a Christian?" she said with a bit of shock. "So am I. And I was praying today that I would meet a Christian woman who could be my friend." Tears poured down her cheek as she tried to get her words out. "Just today I found out that my brother died last night in his sleep. I am so far from home and have had no one to share this with."

We couldn't believe what we were hearing! My friend and I continued to talk with her. With compassion for this grieving woman, we encircled her with comfort and prayer. Before she continued to her destination, we all hugged. As happens when we are invited into someone else's life for even a brief while, a stranger became a friend.

While my friend and I had hurried to meet together for breakfast, the Lord had planned a divine appointment for us instead. This young woman needed someone in the world to see her broken heart.

I thought about how fortunate we were to meet this woman and how easily we could've missed her. I was reminded how a well-lived life is one with room to notice, to pause, to experience the exchanges from one heart to another.

She found herself blessing God for her creation, preservation, and all the blessings of this life, but above all for His inestimable Love; out loud; in a burst of acknowledgement.

ELIZABETH VON ARNIM,
THE ENCHANTED APRIL

The Lens of Love

I have been learning how to see the fingerprints of God in the everyday details of my life. My goal over the years has been to notice those God brings my way with a lens to give encouragement, show love, and bring light. It has required a practice of reminding myself to see people in the authentic context of their life stories, to try to understand where they are coming from, to enter into their worlds of thoughts and feelings, and to leave a bit of grace and encouragement when I sense there is an opening. This habit frees us from a critical heart to develop a generous heart of compassion.

While this is a strong way to connect with and minister to people outside the home, I actually started to cultivate this habit with my family when my children moved into their hormonal years of teenagehood. I knew God called me to look beyond their words and attitudes and perceive what they were feeling inside. Then, as they moved into adulthood, I needed to seek to understand and support them, instead of always giving advice, as they spread their wings. Love for and affirmation of their different phases in life, to this day, gives me access to deep friendship with each of them. This love has carried us through many challenging times and continues to strengthen our bond in each season of life.

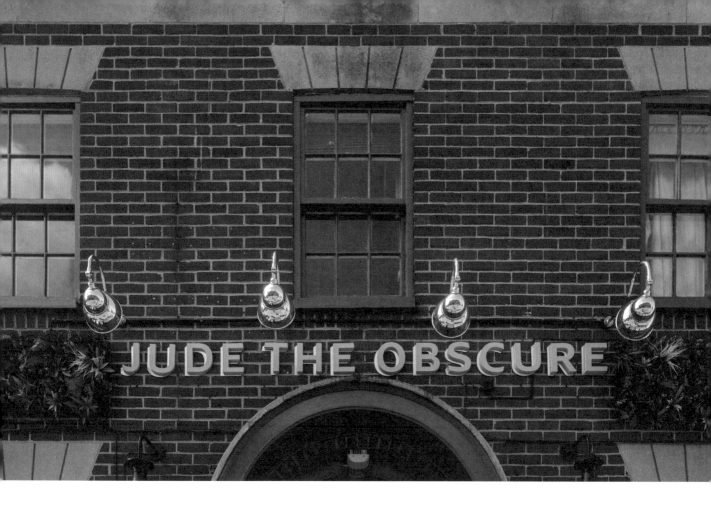

I was reminded how a well-lived life is one
with room to notice, to pause, to experience
the exchanges from one heart to another.

During a beautiful week in the spring, my publishing colleagues were visiting me
to work on a project together. My plan was to take them all around Oxford between

our work and photography sessions each day to show them my favorite cafés, coffee shops, stores, walking paths, and parks so they could see why I loved Oxford so much. I also wanted them to have a good time, so I put thought into the days we would have together. I love to spoil people and find great pleasure in celebrating life with my family, friends, and colleagues.

When I play tour guide to friends, I am given the opportunity to experience the joys of my hometown or favorite places through their eyes. Hopefully it is a fun and interesting time for my guests to have insight into how we make a life and also refreshes our perspective: We notice what we may have walked by hundreds of times or taken for granted, and our gratitude for living in Oxford is renewed.

Everywhere we went together, I chatted with those we encountered. I would greet a barista and ask about her baby girl, or tell a store manager how much his store and fresh produce brought me such pleasure. And as I was walking down the street, a friend called out, "Hey, Sally, how are you?" We talked for a few minutes, he told me of his upcoming marriage, and I was thrilled to hear the details. These are my friends, my neighbors, my community where I live.

The cure for all the ills and wrongs, the cares, the sorrows, and the crimes of humanity, all lie in that one word "love." It is the divine vitality that everywhere produces and restores life. To each and every one of us, it gives the power of working miracles if we will.

LYDIA M. CHILD

*To get the full value
of a joy you must
have somebody to
divide it with.*

MARK TWAIN

My visitors even ended up sharing a meal with each of my children at different times, and I managed to introduce them to my grandchildren—the cutest in all the world, by the way. It was such a personally fulfilling week, made more special by the gift of fellowship.

On our last evening together, we were gathered in a charming restaurant munching on fish and chips when my guests commented on how many people I knew and seemed to enjoy. I was surprised. Didn't everyone reach out to people in their neighborhoods? I found so many ready to be my friend as I walked around town and frequented the local businesses and public spaces. If I hit the ball of friendship, so to speak, to their side of the court, most hit it back.

I shared my perspective with them. Oxford is a place filled with people from all over the world. In a single afternoon, I may hear German, Spanish, Polish, Chinese, and many languages I don't recognize. When people move internationally, it's much harder to find comfort, belonging, and friendship because the values and backgrounds of people can be so different. Loneliness and isolation seem prevalent in many circles. So I was especially grateful that many years ago, I had been challenged to become intentional about the lens through which I viewed my life and the people in it: love.

The Ministry of Love

Years ago I made a point of studying verses in the Bible about the subject of love and came to a deeper understanding that we are made to thrive when we are loved. Love is as oxygen to our whole being. When people feel seen, belong to a community, and feel loved, they are healthier physically, mentally, and spiritually. The reason some babies fail to thrive is that they are not cuddled, loved, touched. Same with adults—we long for love, friendship, and intimacy, for someone to know us and still love us, to share our burdens and perceive our needs. We are also stronger and healthier if we are giving in-like to others who are our friends.

Jesus told His disciples that the world would recognize them as followers of Christ by the way they loved one another (John 13:35). The same is true for each of us. Our love is our testament of faith in Jesus. And how we love becomes a physical expression of that faith. The longer I studied this in Scripture, the more verses I uncovered. They compelled me to make a life goal to figure out how to love those in my direct context: my family, my neighbors, the local people I saw every day, my colleagues, and those attending my lectures or conferences. Here are some of many that called out to me:

*Let all that you do
be done in love.*
1 CORINTHIANS 16:14 ESV

*And above all these
put on love,
which binds everything
together in perfect harmony.*
COLOSSIANS 3:14 ESV

*Anyone who does not
love does not know God,
because God is love.*
1 JOHN 4:8 ESV

*Greater love has no
one than this, that a
person will lay down
his life for his friends.*
JOHN 15:13

*For God so loved the world,
that he gave his only Son,
that whoever believes in
him should not perish
but have eternal life.*
JOHN 3:16 ESV

I determined to grow in viewing my world as a place that deeply needed to see and feel the love through gestures, meals, words, and friendship and to operate from that knowledge. I wanted to learn how to leave everyone I met with a fragrance of God's love. I came up with five simple ways to practice this as a way of life. This is not rocket science, and there are many other ways to show love, but these are modified from the pages of my journal and are ones that resonate with how I put love into action in my life. Writing down ways to show and *be* love helped me shape simple practices that I continue to be mindful of and carry out in daily life.

Consider looking at your life and the people in it and making a list like this one. So many simple ideas come to mind when we pause to consider how to love our people.

Love bears all things, believes all things, hopes all things, endures all things.

1 CORINTHIANS 13:7 ESV

Learn to give everyone words of love that speak to their personalities and self-values.

Expressing appreciation for and interest in people is a way to build them up and form a true bond. "I am so grateful to have a neighbor like you. You always encourage me." "What a cute dog!" (Dogs seem to open many conversations here!) "You make the best coffee in the neighborhood. I look forward to coming to get my caffeine fix from you every day!" "What a beautiful _____ (baby, garden, home)." Ask questions that give them an opportunity to talk. "I would love to know your story—where you grew up, how you ended up here. Tell me about your family." To a child, "Tell me about the toy you are holding. What is your teddy bear's name?" And, of course, to my children, "You are my treasure from God, and I am so very grateful He gave you to me."

Be present to the people in your life.

Paying attention to someone reminds them they are valued. They matter. I avoid looking at my phone or being preoccupied when I am engaging with someone and instead choose to practice looking into the person's eyes to see what might be going on in their heart. Seek to smile at them and show you are glad they are with you…tousling the head of a child, hugging a friend when she is forlorn.

Connect through gifts of service.

Regularly make cookies, buy a small cake, gather small gifts like candles, cards, and fresh flowers, or fix a meal to give to neighbors and friends. I often make treats and meals for those attending my Bible study as a token of friendship. Food and a warm drink always seem to invite deeper conversation.

Notice when others need help and offer that help.

Volunteer to do a neighborly favor, care for a child when a mama needs time to go to the doctor, or reach out to meet up when single friends need a cuppa and some TLC. Make that hard call when someone you know is struggling or has experienced loss. What you say doesn't have to be perfect. Just reaching out and listening will be of great support in their journey.

Invite people to spend time together.

Extend the offer of fellowship and conversation to a new acquaintance or a friend you haven't seen in a while. I invite friends to have coffee, walk on the canals, stroll through the parks, or have breakfast at my house where we can have privacy.

When I was younger, taking initiative almost always seemed to be the way I had to start a friendship—few people ever initiated with me. That experience motivated me to reach out to others and help them feel welcome and appreciated.

I wanted to learn how to leave everyone I met with a fragrance of God's love.

Created for Fellowship

A few years ago, I put out a notice on Facebook that I was coming to Oxford and asked if anyone wanted to meet me at C.S. Lewis's home for a gathering. I ended up with 40 people. One charming woman reached out to me personally and we ended up

getting together periodically. Eventually she became one of my dearest friends, took me on "Tuesday-morning adventures," and spoiled, encouraged, and served me in so many ways. She modeled to me what I needed to do for others. Jacqui makes me laugh, brings me flowers, writes me cards, and even helped me when I was recuperating from hip surgery. Friends like her have held me through dark seasons, believed in me when I needed hope, and shared my deep secrets when I longed for companionship. Our friendship was not one-sided, but reciprocal.

Her friendship modeled for me what I needed to do to others.

Recently I received a note from another friend in my inbox. "Sally, would you have time to meet with me this week?" I am fortunate to have met wonderful women in my Bible studies and through teaching, and I meet with several each week for one-on-one time.

A private table in the corner of one of my favorite cafés was an inviting place for us to have a quiet conversation away from the crowds. After brief chitchat to catch up on life details, my friend's eyes filled with tears. "I just needed to talk to you today. I'm so very lonely. It hurts deeply in a way I can't seem to get beyond. This is a longtime issue for me. I don't feel like I fit in with the normal group. I initiate with many people, inviting them for coffee or to my house for dinner, and we will get together once, but no one asks me back. I feel so silly to not be able to get beyond this, but I wondered if you could help me figure out if in some way I am offensive or hard to get to know."

I should have been surprised. The woman in front of me was accomplished, put together, loving. She was the type who could always be counted on to bring a dessert or some amazing chocolates to share with the group I had been teaching for the last months. She was reliable, fun, and an encouragement to me. But I wasn't surprised because I have received literally hundreds of letters from women expressing the same thing in the past couple of years. Since the pandemic, women were feeling more alone, more disconnected and alienated from others.

It is not true that love makes all things easy, it makes us choose what is difficult.

GEORGE ELIOT

Even in a town like Oxford that overflows with crowds in restaurants and parks, people find themselves feeling isolated and unseen.

It is not the habit of most to reach out. Many people feel ill-equipped to invite others into their lives, to share shame, hurts, fears, or feelings of failure. As a matter of fact, loneliness is such a mental health issue here, creating depression, suicide, drug addiction, that the British government created a position of minister of loneliness because

Behold, Lord,
an empty vessel that
needs to be filled.
My Lord, fill it.
I am weak in the faith,
strengthen me.
I am cold in love; warm
me and make me fervent
That my love may go
out to my neighbor.
Amen.

MARTIN LUTHER

depression had grown to such a degree that it was considered epidemic. This urgency to address loneliness is true in America as well.

Our need for love and friendship is universal. God created us for deep and sweet fellowship. It is a basic need that must be met or health issues will eventually develop. Love is not frivolous; it is essential. Being known and loved is a deep desire to all of us. Just a simple invitation may be just what some need to ease their loneliness and embark on what could become a deep and lifelong friendship. You never know when one of your best life friends is just waiting to have close companionship with you right where you are.

A cup of tea, anyone?

If nature has made you for a giver, your hands are born open, and so is your heart; and though there may be times when your hands are empty, your heart is always full, and you can give things out of that—warm things, kind things, sweet things— help and comfort and laughter—and sometimes gay, kind laughter is the best help of all.

FRANCES HODGSON BURNETT, *A LITTLE PRINCESS*

TEN

WITH ALL OUR HEARTS

*You shall love the L*ORD *your God with all your heart*
and with all your soul and with all your strength.

DEUTERONOMY 6:5

Covid wreaked havoc for almost all of us in some way, robbing from us a centered, satisfying life. For over two years, I longed to visit my son Nathan and his wife in New York City, to be with them in their place, to taste what they savored in this vibrant city. When my husband and I started living for several months out of the year in Oxford we assumed we would make trips throughout Europe, take excursions to historical and interesting places in the UK, and enjoy some freedom as we moved toward retirement. But the travel regulations enacted for pandemic management kept us from taking regional vacations, let alone flying back to New York City to be with our children. Every time I attempted to plan a trip to see my son and his wife, it was thwarted by travel restrictions.

Finally, two and a half years in, I was able to plan a stopover in the Big Apple in December on my way back to Colorado. I was as excited as a little girl at Christmas. Always, there was adventure, fun, and the most satisfying friendship time with these two precious ones.

One afternoon before the trip my phone rang. It was Nathan. "Mama, you'll never guess what! I've been wondering how I could plan a special celebration for us. I know you loved the movie *Funny Girl*. I managed to secure tickets to the musical on Broadway. It's the hottest show around because Lea Michele is playing the main role. They say she's phenomenal. We couldn't get seats together because it's practically sold out, but I got you one fairly close to the front. I think you'll love it."

What a spectacular surprise! I was in awe that he was able to get us tickets. I couldn't imagine anyone better than Barbara Streisand playing the part of Fanny Brice in this epic role, but I had read articles about how dazzling Lea was in the show. I knew it would be fabulous.

On the evening of the play, bustling crowds gathering to see the spectacular Christmas tree in Rockefeller Center and the lights in Times Square swarmed around us as we slowly pushed our way to the theater. Crowds of people stood in line at the ticket office as they waited to get inside to the warmth and find their seats.

As the curtain rose, Lea Michele stepped into her role with energy, enthusiasm, and a generous sparkle that emerged from the bottom of her toes to the top of her head. She filled the stage with her dynamic focus and gave her all to every note she sang, every word she spoke, every scene she graced. She played her part fully, *with all of her heart.*

Rarely have I seen or known such a picture of engaging fully in the moment, giving it her all, spreading her dynamic love for life to hundreds of people at once. It became a memory I will never forget.

What an evening we all celebrated together. We only have one life in which to live fully into each day, each moment with all our hearts.

From the Heart

Early in my professional career, I coached many a winning team of debaters and produced plays with students in the classes I taught. "Fill the stage; sparkle with all the energy you can

muster; reach the person in the very back row of the auditorium with your energy, your eyes, your voice" was a sort of mantra my students heard repeated. Even my children heard this over and again when we shared our messages at our conferences through the years as they were growing up. I wanted them to give their all, their whole heart to their endeavors and in the use of their gifts and blessings.

In my book titled *Dancing with My Heavenly Father*, I pictured God leading me in the great dance of life, teaching me the footsteps, providing the music, the energy, the way. I had discovered that the Bible mentions the word *heart* over 800 times. When we are devoted to wholeheartedly living into God's love, wisdom, truth, virtue, creativity, and artistry, we are moving in the direction of what He desired for us from the beginning.

Proverbs 4:23 tells us, "Above all else, guard your heart, for everything you do flows from it" (NIV). Everything! Our lives are not about following all the right rules, living a moralistic life, "being good" as much as possible. But we are only fully alive when we are connected to God deeply from our heart. Living well, He said, is about relationship, joy in companionship with Him, and enjoying what He has created for our pleasure—everything from mysterious beauty, nature's wonder, faithful friendship, the antics of a puppy, the cuddles of a baby, the kiss of love. God created us to explore His infinite attributes through eternity, singing, praising, playing, enjoying—with all our heart.

So give yourselves completely to God.

JAMES 4:7 NCV

A Satisfied Soul

"Isn't there more to life?"

One foggy evening a friend was walking with me when she asked this question and shared something heavy on her heart. "I thought if I finished my PhD at Oxford, I would find some kind of magical satisfaction by accomplishing something great. Yet now that I have accomplished this, I wonder, what is my life really about? I still have holes in my heart."

I have thought about this often in my years here because people from all over the world say to me, "I would love to live in Oxford as you do. It would be my dream. Life would be so exciting there." Yet, in my experience, Oxford does not make a person happy, fulfill unrealized dreams, or satisfy the soul. Being in a lovely or exciting place can placate our deep desires for a while, but only living into our divine purpose, committing to loving relationships, and basking in the light of God's truth can help us find the belonging and fulfillment we long for. Only God can lead us to this.

*This is what the L*ORD *says: "Let no wise man boast of his wisdom, nor let the mighty man boast of his might, nor a rich man boast of his riches; but let the one who boasts boast of this, that he understands and knows Me, that I am the L*ORD *who exercises mercy, justice, and righteousness on the earth; for I delight in these things," declares the L*ORD*.*

JEREMIAH 9:23-24

Mankind seeks to find fulfillment through academic accomplishment (wisdom), power or influence (might), and wealth and possessions (riches). How many of us at one point or another thought, *If I could just amass these things, I would be happy?*

Yet Jeremiah tells us these are vain pursuits. They are empty of what matters. And my experience reflects this truth: I have rarely met people who found deep satisfaction by pursuing and obtaining those worldly measures of success. In fact, they are often somewhat disappointed, feel disillusioned, or carry regret, bitterness, or cynicism.

God, on the other hand, tells us to love the Lord with *all* our heart.

The human heart must have satisfaction, but there is only one Being who can satisfy the last aching abyss of the human heart, and that is the Lord Jesus Christ.

OSWALD CHAMBERS

This is not an admonition from God because of a religious work God wants us to do; the broader application is that when we do what God has designed us to do, we find what we were looking for: an intimate and loving relationship that satisfies our longing, consistent thoughts that guide us into wisdom and peace, and a healthy life that brings us strength through all of our days. God says He wants us to understand and know Him—the very words I have

communicated to Clay to express my desire to be understood and known to my depths by him. This is the quality of a wholehearted relationship between people and between ourselves and God.

Only living into our divine purpose, committing to loving relationships, and basking in the light of God's truth can help us find the belonging and fulfillment we long for. Only God can lead us to this.

Giving Our All for God

Each of us longs to be a part of an epic story, of a great cause. We want assurance that our lives matter, that we make a difference, that right choices aren't just for the sake of duty. We bargain that we can exist within the mundane moments of singleness, motherhood, marriage, or work if we know and understand that somehow it is meaningful to our overarching life story and heritage. We work to build a story worthy of passing on to others each time we sacrifice to serve or give of our energy to meet the needs of others.

Those efforts have goodness, but if our purposes are not made by seeking Him in the midst of our circumstances,

Have a purpose in life, and, having it, throw such strength of mind and muscle into your work as God has given you.

THOMAS CARLYLE

we are subject to live mundane lives without the presence of His reality, guidance, and treasures of wisdom, blessing, and comfort.

In our performance-oriented world, we tend to measure our sense of worth by what we have accomplished and also by how our accomplishments are acknowledged by others. It becomes the modern way of knowing someone cares about our sacrifices and the investment of our time.

Yet sometimes true accomplishment and worth will not be noticed in this world. Another difficult truth to accept some days is that most of us will never be quite as accomplished as those who are famous, as wealthy, as influential, as popular. Seeking first the kingdom values of God and giving this pursuit our whole heart is how we will find our way.

While we seek His kingdom, what exactly is God looking for within us? Lea Michele embodied what I have aspired to do my whole life: to live as fully as possible into the moment, to learn to give 100 percent, to dance with all my might, as David did (2 Samuel 6:14 NIV). David, the great king in the Old Testament, was a man with flaws and failures common to humans. Yet, in the book of Acts, God gives us insight into what He is really looking for: "I have found David, the son of Jesse, a man after My heart, who will do all My will" (13:22).

David was a child, a mere shepherd when all of his brothers were in the great Hebrew army. And yet God showed this young, common boy favor, because he was a man after His heart.

Jesus chose mostly common people with willing hearts to become His followers and eventual leaders of the church. Their lives were hidden from the wealthy and accomplished. Yet small, hidden lives are sometimes the most fulfilling. When we live without needing or longing for recognition from others, fulfillment comes through faithful love and friendship given over a lifetime and the cultivation of a home where those who enter from the streams of life find comfort, belonging, faith.

Do not store up for yourselves treasures on earth, where moth and rust destroy, and where thieves break in and steal. But store up for yourselves treasures in heaven, where neither moth nor rust destroys, and where thieves do not break in or steal; for where your treasure is, there your heart will be also.

MATTHEW 6:19-21

But from there you will seek the Lord your God, and you will find Him if you search for Him with all your heart and all your soul.

DEUTERONOMY 4:29

My most fulfilling experiences are sitting casually with our family over a meal and celebrating our deep belonging to one another, our true friendships that came about through infinite hidden days of cultivating love, training hearts, and creating life-giving beauty over and over again through ordinary moments of our days.

Now I understand God desires us to love Him with our whole heart because making Him our priority, our "pearl of great price," will build our relationship with Him and others through all the seasons of life. Since there are over 800 verses in the Bible that focus on the heart, we know that God looks at our heart attitudes as the most important channel for growing in love toward Him and our people.

Our Creator's philosophy of shaping us to have a life that reflects the reality and attributes of Christ has more focus on our hearts than our performance and obedience to rules.

Trusting and worshipping God when we understand and when we do not is the only way we will follow His pathways and live by faith in His goodness, even when we are walking through darkness. And with our whole hearts we will keep choosing faith and faithfulness and find that His love is secure and His wisdom in the ways He leads us is always true.

Seeking first the kingdom values of God and giving this pursuit our whole heart is how we will find our way.

I look back through my 70 years of choosing to follow Him *with my whole heart*, and my life has been filled with deep, satisfying relationships and love, meaningful moments touched by the hand of God, open doors that I never could have imagined, and blessings beyond what I knew I could experience from a supernatural, infinite God who had eternal treasures to bestow. Sometimes it meant taking steps forward when I did not know what was ahead. Other times it required waiting to find answers to prayer and learning to strain toward Him. I found all along He was there, ready as a loving Father to bless me, His own precious child.

Our way to this fruitful, flourishing, well-lived life comes when we willingly accept the mantle of devotion with a servant's heart full of love for Him—creating beauty again and again, loving, forgiving, sacrificing, pouring our lives out to bring light and redemption to our world every day. It is then that our lives begin to make sense. Our satisfaction and fulfillment flow from love given and obedience demonstrated in big and small areas. Our unfettered commitment will shine through the blessings of our life and leave a lasting legacy, a story worth telling. The gifts of a well-lived life take the stage when we are finally willing and wanting to please Him with our whole heart.

Lord, because You have me,
I owe You the whole of my love;
Because You have redeemed me,
I owe You the whole of myself;
Because You have promised so much,
I owe You my whole being...
I pray You, Lord, make me taste by love
what I taste by knowledge;
Let me know by love
what I know by understanding.
I owe You more than my whole self,
but I have no more,
And by myself I cannot render
the whole of it to You.
Draw me to You, Lord,
in the fullness of Your love.
I am wholly Yours by creation;
make me all Yours, too, in love.
Amen.

ST. ANSELM

MY FRIEND...

*I hope you have enjoyed my wanderings
and pondering through Oxford.
I pray that as you walk your own path of life,
you will find grace and beauty at each turn.
I leave you with a blessing for your
journey to a well-lived life.*

*May God's hand hold yours each step of the way.
May His deep love fill your heart to
overflowing and encourage your spirit.
May His beauty inspire you and usher in
delight every season.
May His wisdom fill your thoughts
and guide you each day.
May His courage embolden you
to face your trials.
May His protection surround you
as you walk through storms.
May His hope and promises lead you
forward to blessing and joy.*

*All the best to you and your loved ones,
Sally Clarkson*

TO OXFORD...

Oxford, you have been generous to me. Your stories inspired me, and the friendships you offered expanded my understanding of people from many different contexts. Walking endless miles in parks, along canals, around meadows was a sort of therapy where I worked out deep thoughts about life. Conversations over thousands of cups of tea and brews of coffee provided nourishment for a deep soul, filling up my heart with treasures of wisdom, truth, and affection. You have taught me some new secrets of a well-lived life. You will live in my heart forever.

ACKNOWLEDGEMENTS

Thanks a million-zillion to Ruth, who so energetically made this project come to life. You are a treasure. So glad we are friends.

And my deep gratitude to the best team of creatives—Lori, Ruth, Hope, and Jacqui—who followed me around Oxford, tirelessly, energetically, enthusiastically without complaint of the thousands of steps we took, and the challenges we faced. I will always be grateful for you and for your friendship.

ABOUT THE AUTHOR

Sally Clarkson is a bestselling author of many books, renowned speaker, and beloved mentor who has dedicated her life to inspiring women worldwide to live for Christ. She especially focuses on making a home, nurturing strong family ties, developing an insightful philosophy of education, and committing to discipleship that transforms lives. Her podcast, *At Home with Sally*, has over 26 million downloads. She has been married to her husband, Clay, for more than 40 years. They have raised four adult children who are her best friends and cherished companions. Her four grandchildren delight her heart to the depths. Today, Sally divides her time between the mountains of Colorado and the rolling fields of England. You can connect with her at SallyClarkson.com.

ABOUT THE PHOTOGRAPHER

Lori Sparkman is an entrepreneur, commercial photographer, and the owner of Lori Sparkman Photography. For more than 15 years she has worked extensively with corporate branding accounts, the fitness industry, weddings, and high-profile clients. Based in Little Rock, Arkansas, Lori is a sought-after traveling photographer and has roamed the world with camera in hand to capture celebrations and special events. Her visual artistry can be seen in local magazines and published books including *Our Wedding Planner* and *Teatime Discipleship*. With a sophisticated and lighthearted style Lori thrives on creative challenges and building strong relationships with the clients who put their trust in her for their most important moments and projects.

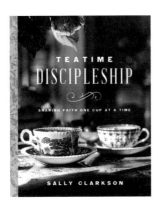

Teatime Discipleship

Sharing Faith One Cup at a Time

With *Teatime Discipleship*, Sally will invite you in, pour you a cup of tea, and share with you what she's learned about how our incredible Lord reveals His glory through our home life, relationships, and daily responsibilities.

Teatime Discipleship for Mothers and Daughters

Pouring Faith, Love, and Beauty into Your Girl's Heart

Teatime Discipleship for Mothers and Daughters will help you steep together in Scripture as you make meaningful time for God and for each other.

Published in association with The Bindery Agency, www.The BinderyAgency.com

For bulk, special sales, or ministry purchases, please call 1-800-547-8979. Email: CustomerService@hhpbooks.com

Cover and interior design by Janelle Coury

Photographs on pages 31, 46, 66, 86, 116, 132, 139, 144, 155, 165, 172, 200, 220 are provided by the Clarkson family

Photographs on pages 87, 198, 201 are from Unsplash

All other photographs & cover image © Lori Sparkman

WELL LIVED

Copyright © 2024 by Sally Clarkson
Published by Harvest House Publishers
Eugene, Oregon 97408
www.harvesthousepublishers.com

ISBN 978-0-7369-8547-5 (hardcover)
ISBN 978-0-7369-8548-2 (eBook)

Printed in China

24 25 26 27 28 29 30 31 32 / RDS / 10 9 8 7 6 5 4 3 2 1